George MacDonald

Parables and ballads and Scotch songs

George MacDonald

Parables and ballads and Scotch songs

ISBN/EAN: 9783744749091

Printed in Europe, USA, Canada, Australia, Japan

Cover: Foto ©Thomas Meinert / pixelio.de

More available books at **www.hansebooks.com**

PARABLES AND BALLADS

AND SCOTCH SONGS

By GEORGE MACDONALD, LL.D.

A NEW EDITION

London
CHATTO & WINDUS PICCADILLY
1891

CONTENTS.

PARABLES:—

THE MAN OF SONGS	
THE HILLS	5
THE JOURNEY	9
THE TREE'S PRAYER	18
WERE I A SKILFUL PAINTER	21
FAR AND NEAR	24
MY ROOM	28
DEATH AND BIRTH	44
LOVE'S ORDEAL	51
THE LOST SOUL	70
THE THREE HORSES	75
THE GOLDEN KEY	88
SOMNIUM MYSTICI	93
THE SANGREAL	126
THE FAILING TRACK	150

PARABLES:—continued.

	Page
Tell Me	152
Brother Artist	156
After an Old Legend	160
A Meditation of St. Eligius	164
The Early Bird	167
Sir Lark and King Sun	171
The Owl and the Bell	174

BALLADS:—

The Unseen Model	183
The Homeless Ghost	188
Abu Midjan	204
The Thankless Lady	221
Legend of the Corrievrechan	224
The Dead Hand	229

SCOTCH SONGS AND BALLADS:—

Annie She's Dowie	235
O Lassie Ayont the Hill!	236
The Bonny, Bonny Dell	240
Jeanie Braw	245

CONTENTS.

SCOTCH SONGS AND BALLADS:—*continued.*

	Page
OWER THE HEDGE	248
GAEIN' AND COMIN'	253
A SANG O' ZION	255
TIME AND TIDE	256
THE WAFSOME CARL	260
THE MERMAID	266
THE YERL O' WATERIDECK	272
THE TWA GORDONS	280
THE LAST WOOIN'	293
ALL SOULS' EVE	299

PARABLES.

B

PARABLES.

THE MAN OF SONGS.

"THOU wanderest in the land of dreams,
    O man of many songs!
To thee what is but looks and seems—
No realm to thee belongs."

"Seest thou those mountains, faint and far,
    O spirit caged and tame?"
"Clouds! clouds! Like distant hills they are,
    But like is not the same."

"Nay, nay! I know them all too well—
Ridge, cliff, and peak, and dome:
In that cloudland, in one high dell,
Nesteth my little home."

THE HILLS.

Behind my father's cottage lies
   A gentle grassy height,
Up which I often ran—to gaze
   Back with a wondering sight;
For on the chimneys I looked down—
   So high—below me quite!

All round, where'er I turned mine eyes,
   Huge hills closed up the view;
The town, 'midst their converging roots,
   Was clasped by rivers two;
From one hill to another sprang
   The sky's great vault of blue.

Oh, how I loved to climb their sides,
   And in the heather lie !
From mighty vantage gazing down
   On the castle grim and high ;
Blue streams below, white clouds above—
   Unmoving in the sky !

And now, wherever I may roam,
   At sight of stranger hill,
A new sense of the old delight
   Springs in my bosom still ;
And longings for the high unknown
   The ancient channels fill.

For I am always climbing hills,
   From the known to the unknown—
Surely, at last, on some high peak,
   To find my Father's throne,

THE HILLS.

Though hitherto I have only found
   His footsteps in the stone.

And in my wanderings once I met
   Another searching too;
The dawning hope, the shared quest
   Our hearts together drew:
She laid her trusting hand in mine,
   Unquestioning and true.

She was not born among the hills,
   Yet on every mountain face
A something known her inward eye
   By inborn light can trace;
For up all hills must homeward be,
   Though no one knows the place.

Clasp my hand close in thine, my child—
   A long way we have come!

Clasp my hand closer yet, my child.
We farther yet must roam—
Climbing and climbing, till we reach
Our heavenly Father's home.

THE JOURNEY.

Hark, the rain is on my roof!
Every murmur, through the dark,
Stings me with a dull reproof,
Like a half-extinguished spark.
It is I! but how come here—
Wide awake and wide alone—
Caught within a net of fear—
All my dreams dreamed out and gone?

I will rise; I will go forth.
Better face the hideous night,
Better dare the harmful north,
Than be mastered with affright!

PARABLES.

Black wind rushing—every blast
Sown with arrowy points of rain!
Time and place are gone and past—
I am here, and so is pain!

. . . .

Dead in dreams the gloomy street!
I will out on open roads.
Eager grow my aimless feet—
Onward, onward something goads.
I will take the mountain path,
Beard the storm within its den;
Know the worst of this dim wrath
Harassing the souls of men.

Chasm 'neath chasm! rock piled on rock
Roots, and crumbling earth, and stones!
Hark, the torrent's thundering shock!
Hark, the swaying pine tree's groans!

THE JOURNEY.

Ah! I faint, I fall, I die—
Sink to nothingness away!—
Lo, a streak upon the sky!
Lo, the opening eye of day!

II.

Mountain summits lift their snows
O'er a valley green and low;
And a winding pathway goes
Guided by the river's flow;
And a music rises ever,
As of peace and low content,
From the pebble-paven river,
Like an odour, upward sent.

And the sound of ancient harms
Moans behind, the hills among,

PARABLES.

Like the humming of the swarms
That unseen the forest throng.
Now I meet the shining rain
From a cloud with sunny weft;
Now against the wind I strain,
Sudden burst from mountain cleft.

Now a sky that hath a moon,
Staining all the cloudy white
With a faded rainbow—soon
Lost in deeps of heavenly night!
Now a morning clear and soft,
Amber on the purple hills;
Warm blue day of summer, oft
Cooled by wandering windy rills!

Joy to travel thus along,
With the universe around!

Every creature of the throng,
Every sight and scent and sound
Homeward speeds with beauty laden,
Beelike, to its hive, my soul!
Mine the eye the stars are made in!
Mine the heart of Nature's whole!

III.

Hills retreat on either hand,
Sinking slowly to the plain;
Solemn through the outspread land
Rolls the river to the main.
As the twilight grows the night,
Something through the dusky air
Doubtful glimmers, faintly white,
But I know not what nor where.

Is it but a chalky ridge,
Bared of sod, like tree of bark?

PARABLES.

Or a river-spanning bridge,
Miles away into the dark?
Or the foremost leaping waves
Of the everlasting sea,
Where the Undivided laves
Time with its eternity?

Is it but an eye-made sight—
In my brain a fancied gleam?
Or a faint aurora-light
From the sun's tired smoking team?
Known shall be the thing unknown,
When the morning climbs the sky:
In the darkness it is gone,
Yet with every step draws nigh.

Onward, onward through the night!
Matters it I cannot see?

THE JOURNEY.

I am moving in a might
Dwelling in the dark and me.
End or way I cannot lose—
Grudge to rest, or fear to roam:
All is well with wanderer whose
Heart is travelling hourly home.

IV.

Joy! O joy! the dawning sea
Answers to the dawning sky;
Foretaste of the coming glee
When the sun will lord it high.
See the swelling radiance grow
To a dazzling glory-might!
Thoughtful shadows gently go
'Twixt the wave tops wild with light!

Hear the smiting billows clang!
See the falling billows lean

Half a watery vault, and hang
Gleaming with translucent green—
Then in thousand fleeces lie,
Thundering light upon the strand! —
Vague it reached my doubting eye
Through the dusk, across the land.

See, a boat! Out, out we dance:
Fierce wind swoops my fluttering sail!
What a terrible expanse—
Tumbling hill and heaving dale!
Restless, helpless, lost I float—
Captive to the lawless free!
And my prison is my boat—
Oh, for petrel-wings to flee!

Look below: each watery whirl
Cast in beauty's living mould!

Look above : each feathery curl
Dropping crimson, dropping gold !
Oh, I tremble in the gush
Of an everlasting youth !
Love and fear together rush :
I am free—in God, the Truth !

THE TREE'S PRAYER.

ALAS, 'tis cold and dark!
The wind has all night sung a wintry tune!
Hail from black clouds that swallowed up the
    moon,
Beat, beat against my bark.

Oh! why delays the spring?
Not yet the sap moves in my frozen veins;
Through all my withered roots creep numbing
    pains,
That I can hardly cling.

THE TREE'S PRAYER.

The sun shone yester-morn;
I felt the glow down every fibre float,
And thought I heard a thrush's piping note,
Of dim dream-gladness born.

Then, on the salt gale driven,
The streaming cloud hissed through my outstretched arms,
Tossed me about in slanting snowy swarms.
And blotted out the heaven.

All night I brood and choose
Among past joys. Oh, for the breath of June!
The feathery light-flakes quavering from the moon!
The slow-baptizing dews!

Oh the joy-frantic birds!—
They are the tongues of us, mute, longing trees!
Aha! the billowy odours! and the bees
That browse like scattered herds!

The comfort-whispering showers,
That thrill with gratefulness my youngest shoot!
The children playing round my deep-sunk root,
Cold-shadowed in hot hours!

See, see the heartless dawn,
With naked, chilly arms latticed across!
Another weary day of moaning loss,
On the thin-shadowed lawn!

But the deep snow is past,
And climbing suns persuade the relenting wind;
I will endure with steadfast patient mind:
My leaves *will* come at last.

WERE I A SKILFUL PAINTER.

Were I a skilful painter,
My pencil, not my pen,
Should try to teach thee hope and fear ;
And who should blame me then ?—
Fear of the tide of darkness
That floweth fast behind,
And hope to make thee journey on
In the journey of the mind.

Were I a skilful painter,
What should I paint for thee ?—
A tiny spring-bud peeping out
From a withered wintry tree.

The warm blue sky of summer
O'er jagged ice and snow,
And water hurrying gladsome out
From a cavern down below.

The dim light of a beacon
Upon a stormy sea,
Where a lonely ship to windward beats,
For life and liberty.
A watery sun-ray gleaming
Athwart a sullen cloud.
Slow dawning peace upon a brow
In angry weeping bowed.

Morn climbing o'er a mountain,
And scattering the night,
And a traveller for the sunny east,
Rejoicing in the sight.

A taper nearly vanished
Amid the dawning gray,
And a maiden lifting up her head,
And lo, the coming day!

Thus, thus, were I a painter,
My pencil, not my pen,
Should try to teach thee hope and fear;
And who should blame me then?—
Fear of the tide of darkness
That floweth fast behind,
And hope to make thee journey on
In the journey of the mind.

FAR AND NEAR.

[The fact which suggested this poem, is related by Dr. Edward Clarke in his Travels.]

I.

Blue sky above blue sea did glow,
    North from the old Nile's mouth—
A world of blue, wherein did blow
    A soft wind from the south.

In great and solemn heaves, the mass
    Of pulsing ocean beat,
Unwrinkled as the sea of glass
    Beneath the holy feet.

With forward leaning of desire,
    The ship sped calmly on,
A pilgrim strong that would not tire,
    Or hasten to be gone.

II.

List!—on the wave!—What can they be,
　Those sounds that hither glide?
No lovers whisper tremulously,
　Under the ship's round side;

No sail across the great blue sphere
　Holds white obedient way;
No far-fled, sharp-winged boat is near,
　No following fish at play.

'Tis not the rippling of the wave,
　Nor sighing of the cords—
No winds or waters ever gave
　A murmur so like words;

Nor wings of birds that northward strain,
    Nor talk of hidden crew:
The traveller questioned, but in vain—
    He found no answer true.

III

A hundred level miles away,
    On Egypt's troubled shore,
Two nations fought, that sunny day.
    With bellowing cannons' roar.

The fluttering whisper, low and near,
    Was that far battle's blare;
A lipping, rippling motion here,
    The blasting thunder there.

IV.

Can this dull sighing in my breast,
   All faint and undefined,
Be the worn edge of far unrest
   Borne on the spirit's wind?

The uproar of high battle fought
   Betwixt the bond and free?
The thunderous roll of armed thought
   Dwarfed to an ache in me?

MY ROOM.

To G. E. M.

'Tis a little room, my friend—
Baby walks from end to end.
All the things look sadly real,
This hot noontide unideal.
Vaporous heat from cope to basement
All you see outside the casement,
Save one house all mud-becrusted,
And a street all drought-bedusted !
See, there comes its happiest vision—
Trickling water-cart's derision !
Shut we out the staring space—
Draw the curtains in its face !

MY ROOM.

Close the eyelids of the room ;
Fill it with a scarlet gloom :
Lo ! the walls with warm flush dyed !
Lo ! the ceiling glorified,
As when, lost in tenderest pinks,
White rose on the red rose thinks !
But beneath, a hue right rosy,
Red as a geranium-posy,
Stains the air with power estranging,
Known with unknown clouding, changing.
See in ruddy atmosphere
Dulness melt and disappear :
Look around on either hand—
Are we not in fairyland ?

On that couch, inwrapt in mist
Of vaporized amethyst,
Lie, as in a rose's heart :
Secret things I would impart.

PARABLES.

Any time you would receive them —
Easier, though, you will believe them,
Bathed in glowing mystery
Of the red light shadowy;
For this ruby-hearted hue,
Sanguine core of all the true
Which for love the heart would plunder,
Is the very hue of wonder;
This dissolving dreamy red
Is the self-same radiance shed
From the heart of poet young,
Like red poppy sunlight-stung;
If in light you make a schism,
'Tis the deepest in the prism.

This poor-seeming room, in fact,
Is of marvels all compact,
So disguised by common daylight,
By its disenchanting gray light,

Only spirit-eyes, mesmeric.
See its beauty esoteric.
Loftiest observatory
Ne'er unveiled such hidden glory;
Never sage's furnace-kitchen
Magic wonders was so rich in—
Never book of wizard old
Clasped such in its iron hold.

See—that case against the wall,
Glowingly purpureal!—
A piano to the prosy;
But to us in twilight rosy—
What?—A cave where Nereids lie,
Naiads, Dryads, Oreads sigh,
Dreaming of the time when they
Danced in forest and in bay.
In that chest before your eyes,
Nature self-enchanted lies;—

PARABLES.

Awful hills and midnight woods;
Sunny rains in solitudes;
Babbling streams in forests hoar·
Seven-hued icebergs; oceans frore.--
See them? No; I said *enchanted*—·
That is—hid away till wanted.
Do you hear a voice of singing?
That is Nature's priestess flinging
Spells around her baby's riot,
Binding it in moveless quiet :—
She at will can disenchant them,
And to prayer believing grant them.

Do you doubt me? Soon will night
Free her hands for fair delight:
Then invoke her—she will come.
Fold your arms, be blind and dumb.
She will bring a book of spells
Writ like crabbed oracles :

Like Sabrina's. will her hands
Thaw the power of charmed bands;
First will music loosened rush
Round thee in a glorious gush;
Next, upon its waves will sally,
Like a stream-god down a valley,
Nature's self, the formless former,
Nature's self, the peaceful stormer—
Enter thee, and captive take thee,
And both one and many make thee—
One by softest power to still thee,
Many by the thoughts that fill thee. —
Let me make three guesses where
She her prisoner will bear.

On a mountain-top you stand,
Gazing o'er a sunny land;
Shining streams, like silver veins,
Rise in dells and meet in plains;

Up yon brook, a hollow lies,
Dumb as love that fears surprise :
Moorland tracts of broken ground
O'er it rise and close it round :
He who climbs from bosky dale
Hears the foggy breezes wail.
Yes, thou know'st the nest of love—
Know'st as well the waste above !
But, or type or pictured past,
As it dawns it fades as fast—
In thy sadness fades away
To a misty gloom of gray.

Sinks the sadness into rest,
Ripple-like on water's breast ;
Mother's bosom rests the daughter—
Grief the ripple, love the water ;
And thy brain like wind-harp lies,
Breathed upon from distant skies ;

MY ROOM.

Till, soft-gathering, visions new
Grow like vapours in the blue;
White forms, flushing hyacinthine.
Move in curvings labyrinthine;
With an airy wishful gait,
On the counter-motion wait;
And with godlike graceful feet,
For such mazy marvelling meet,
Press from air a shining sound,
Rippling after, lingering round;
Hair afloat and arms aloft
Fill the chord of movement soft.

Gone the measure polyhedral!
Towers aloft a fair cathedral;
Every arch—like praying arms
Upward flung in love's alarms,
Knit by clasped hands o'erhead—
Heaves to heaven a weight of dread;

PARABLES.

In thee, like an angel-crowd,
Grows the music, praying loud;
Swells thy spirit with devotion,
As a strong wind swells the ocean;
Sweeps the visioned pile away—
Leaves thy heart alone, to pray.

Then the prayer grows dim and dies,
Like a sunset from the skies;
Comes another change of mood
O'er thy inner solitude:
Growing, growing, tone by tone—
Lo, thyself magician grown!
Walking open-eyed through earth,
To behold the dawning birth
Of a thousand marvellous things,
Which in darkness have their springs:
Half thou seëst whence they flow—
Half thou seëst whither go;

Nature's consciousness, whereby
On herself she turns her eye,
Thou for her, all men and thee,
Hopest coming harmony.

But I turn; for when the sun
Leaves the glowing curtain dun,
I, of prophet-insight reft,
Shall be dull and dreamless left,
And must therefore hasten proof,
Weaving in the warp my woof.

What are those upon the wall,
Ranged in rows symmetrical?
Of those now, if you have patience,
I would offer revelations:—
Through the wall of things external
Posterns they to the supernal;
Through locked gates of place and time,

Wickets to the eternal prime
Lying round the noisy day,
Full of silences alway—
Lying round the darksome night,
Full of awful shining light.

That, my friend? Now, it is curious,
You should hit upon the spurious!
'Tis a door to nowhere, that;
Throw it open, wide and flat,
You will see the wall's expanse—
Hung with cobweb ignorance.

Do not open that one so;
Wait until the sun is low.
If you careless lift its latch,
Not a glimmer you will catch
Mere negation, blank of hue,
Out of it will stare at you.

Wait, I say, the coming night—
Fitter time for thinking sight,
When the wide eyes of the mind
See far down the spirit's wind.
You may have to push and pull,
Force and lift with many a tool,
Ere the rugged, ill-joined door
Yield the sight it stands before;
But at length, with dawning sweep,
Wide it swings—and lo, the deep!

Thou art standing on the verge
Where things visible emerge!
On thy joy-astonished eyes
Mountain-splendours awful rise!
Hoary silence, lightning-fleet,
Shooteth hellward at thy feet!
Fear not, thou whose life is truth—
Gazing will renew thy youth;

But if sin of soul or flesh
One should hold in snaring mesh.
It will drag him through the door,
Him to windy fate give o'er—
Ages to be blown and hurled
Up and down a limbo-world.

Ah! your eyes ask how I brook
Doors that are not, doors to look!
That is whither I was tending,
And it brings me to good ending.

Baby is the cause of this;
Odd it seems, but so it is.—
Baby, with her pretty prate,
Molten, half articulate,
Full of hints, suggestions, catches,
Broken verse, and music snatches,
Like an angel gone astray,

Must be taught the homeward way;
Plant of heaven, she, rooted lowly,
Must put forth a blossom holy,
Must, with culture high and steady,
Slow unfold a gracious lady;
We must keep her full of wonder
At the daisy and the thunder,
At the moon and stars and sea,
At the butterfly and bee;
Never her and childhood part,
Change the brain, but keep the heart.
So, from lips and hands and looks,
She must learn to honour books,
Yet must learn that mere *appearing*
Gives no title to revering;
That a pump is not a well,
Nor a priest an oracle:
Sight convincing to her mind,
I will separate kind from kind,

And those books, though honoured by her,
Gently lay upon the fire;
Sacred form even shall not hinder
Their consumption to a cinder.

Would you see the slight immortal,
One short pace within our portal?
I will fetch her.—See how white!
Solemn pure—a light in light!
Gleaming frock and lily-skin
White as whitest ermelin
Washed in palest thinnest rose!
Like a thought of God she goes,
Wandering ever in the dance
Of her own sweet radiance:
Books and music far asunder—
Of all wonders, she's the wonder!

But, my friend, I've rattled plenty

MY ROOM.

To suffice for mornings twenty.
I should never stop of course,
Therefore stop I will perforce.—
Did I lead them up, choragic,
To reveal their nature magic,
Twenty things, past contradiction,
Yet would prove I spoke no fiction
Of the room's belongings cryptic
Read by light apocalyptic.
There is that machine, glass-masked,
With continual questions tasked,
Ticking with untiring rock :
It is called an eight-day clock ;
But to me the thing appears
Made for winding up the years ;
Yes, thank God, fast as it may,
On it draws a mighty day.

DEATH AND BIRTH.

'Tis the midnight hour—I heard
Chiming bells give out the word.
Seldom is the lamp-ray shed
On a quick foot-farer's head,
Where the tall and narrow street
Stretches far below my feet.
Lone I sit at lattice old,
Gazing into dark and cold.

See—her windows, every story,
Shine—a far-off nebulous glory!
All within that luminous cloud,
Planet-stars like atoms crowd—

DEATH AND BIRTH.

Flashing jewels, flashing eyes,
In a mist of rainbow-dyes.
In her orbs' victorious lightning,
See the others paling, brightening!
Those on which they gracious turn —
Stars combust — all tenfold burn;
Those from which they turn away,
Listless roam in twilight gray.
When on her my looks I bent,
Wonder shook me like a tent,
And my eyes grew dim with sheen,
Wasting light upon its queen.
But though she my eyes might chain,
Rule my ebbing flowing brain,
Truth alone, without, within,
Can the soul's high homage win.

He, I doubt not, too is there,
Who unveiled my idol fair;

PARABLES.

And I thank him, grateful much.
Though his end was none of such.
He from shapely lips of wit
Let the fire-flakes lightly flit,
Scorching as the snow that fell
On the damned in Dante's hell;
With keen-worded opposition,
Playful, merciless precision,
Mocked the sweet romance of youth,
Balancing on spheric truth;
He on sense's firm set plane
Rolled the unstable ball amain:
With a smile she looked at me—
Stung my soul, and set me free.

Ah! come in; I need your aid.
Tools—you've brought them, as I said?—
The material of your calling—
Stone and lime, dressed, mixed, for walling?

There, my friend, build up that niche—
That one with the painting rich.—
Yes, you're right; it is a show
Picture seldom can bestow;
City palaces and towers,
Terraced gardens, twilight bowers,
Vistas deep through swaying masts,
Pennons flaunting in the blasts.—
Yes, a window you would call it;
Not the less up you must wall it.
In that niche the dead world lies—
Bury death, and free mine eyes.

Youths who lately held by me,
Said I taught, yet left you free,
Hold to what I taught you then.
Ah, no, no! as ye are men,
Find the secret—follow and find;
All forget that lies behind;

PARABLES.

Me, yourselves, the schools forsake:
In your souls a silence make;
Hearken till a whisper come;
Listen, follow, and be dumb.

There! 'tis over; I am dead!
Of the past the broken thread
Only holding in my hand.
O my soul—the merry land!
On my heart, like falling vault,
All the ruining past makes halt;
Ages I could sit and moan
For the something that is gone.

Haste and pierce the other wall!
Break an opening to the All!
Where? I care not; quickest best.
Kind of window? Let that rest:

Who at morning ever lies
Thinking how to ope his eyes?

It were well, of course, to fall
On the thinnest of the wall ;—
There is what you call a niche.—
No ; this—better far—in which
Stands the Crucifix. You start ?—
Ah, you half-believing heart !
Reverently, the marble cold
In my living arms I fold
—Thou, the window of the land,
Wouldst not have thy dead form stand
Shutting out the wind and sky,
And the dayspring from on high !
Brother with the rugged crown,
Gently thus I lift thee down.

I will take your tool, and do

What I can to drive it through.
Yes; I have but little skill,
But I have a hearty will.

   Stroke on stroke! The frescoed plaster
Clashes downward, fast and faster.
Hark! I heard an outer stone
Down the rough rock rumbling thrown
Filters through a sickly beam!
Struggles through an airy stream!
Lo!—the mass is outward flung!
In the universe hath sprung!

   See the gold upon the blue,
Where the sun comes blinding through!
See the far-off mountain shine
In the dazzling light divine!
Gloomy world, thy reign is done!
Welcome wind and sky and sun!

LOVE'S ORDEAL.

A RECOLLECTION AND ATTEMPTED COMPLETION OF A PROSE FRAGMENT READ IN CHILDHOOD.

"HEAR'ST thou that sound upon the window
    pane?"
Said the youth softly, as outstretched he lay
Where for an hour outstretched he had lain—
Softly, yet with a tone of half dismay.
Answered the maiden: "It is but the rain,
Which has been gathering in the west all day.
Why shouldst thou hearken so? Thine eyelids
    close,
And let me gather peace from thy repose."

"Hear'st thou that moan, creeping along the
	ground?"
Said the youth, and his veiling eyelids rose
From deeps of lightning-haunted dark profound,
Ruffled with herald blasts of coming woes.
"I hear it," said the maiden; "'tis the sound
Of a great wind that here not seldom blows;
It swings the huge arms of the dreary pine;
But thou art safe, my darling, clasped in mine."

"Hear'st thou the baying of my hounds?"
	said he;
"Draw back the lattice bar and let them in."
Through a rent cloud the moon-light, ghostily,
Fell on the cottage floor; and, gaunt and thin,
With one leap stood the stag-hounds by his knee,
Shaking the rain-drops from their shaggy skin.
The maiden closed the rain-bespattered glass,
Whose spotted shadow through the room did pass.

The youth, half-raised, was leaning on his
    hand,
But when again beside him sat the maid,
His eyes for one slow minute having scanned
Her thoughtful face, he laid him down, and said,
Monotonous, like solemn-read command :
" For love is of the earth, earthy, and is laid
At length back lifeless in its mother's womb."
Strange moanings from the pine-tree crossed the
    gloom ;

And yet again two shadows like of glass,
Over the moonbeams on the cottage floor,
As wind almost as thin and shapeless, pass ;
A sound of rain-drops came about the door,
And a soft sighing as of plumy grass ;
A look of sorrowing doubt the youth's face wore ;
The two great hounds half-rose, with aspect grim,
And eyed his countenance by the taper dim.

But not one sight or sound the maiden noted;
Her heart was in the half-reproachful look
Which doubted whether he the saying had quoted
Out of some evil, earth-begotten book,
Or up, from great slow depths, like bubbles had
    floated
Words which no maiden ever yet could brook;
But his eyes held the question—" Yea or No?"
Therefore the maiden answered: " Nay, not so;

" Love is of heaven, eternal." Half a smile
Just twinned his lips: shy, like all human best,
A hopeful thought bloomed out, and lived a
    while;
Slow, softly, sunk his head upon her breast,
Like a tossed bark that in a sunny isle
At length has found the haven of its rest,
But cannot long remain, must forward fare:
Soon raising it, he said, with words too bare,

"Maiden, I have loved other maidens." Pale
Her red lips grew. "I loved them—yes—but they,
One after one, in trial's hour did fail;
For after sunset, clouds again are gray."
A sudden light shone through the fringy veil
That drooping hid her eyes; and then there lay
A stillness on her face, waiting; and then
The little clock rung out the hour of ten.

Moaning once more the great pine-branches bow—
Moan vexed, because the wind in vain they stem.
Brooding upon her face, the youth said—"Thou
Art not more beautiful than some of them,
But well-willed hoping crowns thy peaceful brow;
Nor glow thine eyes, but shine serene, like gem
That lamps from radiant store upon the dark
The light it gathered where its song the lark.

"The horse that broke this day from grasp of
    three,
Thou sawest then the hand thou holdest, hold:
Ere two fleet hours are gone, that hand will be
Dry, big-veined, wrinkled, withered up and old!
I say no more—judge thou the doom I dree."
With calm fixed eyes she listened as he told;
The stag-hounds rose, a little gazed at him,
Then sunk their heads, and growled a purpose
    grim.

    Spake on the youth, nor altered look or tone:
"Maiden, I have a fearful thing to bear—"
Was it the maiden's, that importunate moan?—
"At midnight, when the moon sets: wilt thou dare
Go with me, dear, or must I go alone
To meet an agony that will not spare?"
She answered not, but rose, and caught her cloak:
He staying her, glad-eyed, on further spoke.

"Not yet," he said; "yet there is respite;
   see,
Time's rope must make two coils before the hour;
Yet is the time too short for telling thee
My tale from far beginnings, whence the power
Of the great dark that shadows down on me:
Red roses cluster all my love's dear bower—
Nightshade and hemlock, darnel, toadstools white
Compass the place where I must lie to-night.

  Around his neck the maiden put her arm,
And knelt beside, half leaning on his breast;
As o'er his love, to keep it strong and warm,
Brooding like bird outspread upon her nest.
And well the faith of such dear eyes might charm
All doubt and fear to love's primeval rest!
He drew her face upon his heart, and then
Spake on with voice like wind in lonely glen.

A drearier howling through the pine did go,
Which, as with human voice, complained and
    cried
For one long minute; then the sound grew slow,
Sunk to a moan, and moaning sunk and died.
Two voices only now the silence mow—
His, and the clock's grown loud, which did
    divide
The hours into live moments—sparks of time,
Scorching the soul that watches for the chime.

He spoke of sins ancestral, born in him;
Of long resistance and despairings wild;
Of strength reviving choked in questions dim;
Of lonesome dreariness love-unbeguiled;
Of storm, and blasting light, and darkness grim;
Of torrent paths, and tombs with mountains piled;
Of gulfs in the unsunned bosom of the earth;
Of dying ever into dawning birth.

"But when I find a heart whose blood is wine;
Whose faith lights up the cold brain's passionless
    hour;
Whose love, like unborn rose-bud, will not pine,
But wait the sun and the baptizing shower—
Till then lies hid, and gathers odours fine
To greet the human summer, when its flower
Shall blossom in the heart and soul and brain,
And love and passion be one holy twain—

"Then shall I rest—rest like the seven of yore;
Slumber divine shall steep my outworn soul,
And every stain dissolve to the very core.
She too shall slumber, having found her goal.
Time's ocean o'er us will, in silence frore,
A thousand tides of change-filled seasons roll,
And its long, dark, appointed period fill.
Then shall we wake together, loving still."

Her face on his, her mouth to his mouth pressed,
Was all the answer of the trusting maid.
Close in his arms he held her to his breast
For one brief moment—would have yet assayed
Some deeper word her heart to strengthen, lest
It should though faithful be too much afraid;
But the clock gave the warning to the hour—
And on the thatch fell sounds not of a shower.

One long kiss, and the maiden rose. A fear
Lay, thin as a glassy shadow, on her heart;
She quivered as some unknown thing were near,
But smiled next moment—for they should not part.
Next rose the youth. With solemn-joyous cheer,
He helped the maid, whose trembling hands did thwart
Her haste—and wrapped her in her mantle's fold.
Then out they passed into the midnight cold.

The moon was sinking in the dim green west,
Curled upwards from the steep horizon's brink,
A leaf of glory falling to its rest.
The maiden's hand, still trembling, sought to link
Her arm to his, with love's instinctive quest,
But his arm folded her lest she should sink;
And so her hand, set free, stole him around,
And they walked thus in freedom's fetters bound.

Pressed to his side, she felt, like full-toned bell,
A mighty heart heave large in measured play;
But as the floating moon aye lower fell,
Its bounding force did, by slow loss, decay.
Now like a throbbing bird! now like a knell
Afar and faint! And now, with sick dismay,
She felt the arm relax that round her clung,
And from her circling arm he forward hung.

His footsteps feeble, short his paces grow :
Her strength and courage mount and swell amain.
He lifted up his head : the moon lay low,
Nigh the world's edge.   His lips with some keen
    pain
Quivered, but with a smile his eyes turned slow,
Seeking in hers a balsam for his bane,
And found it—love, o'er terror all-supreme.
Like two sad souls they walked met in one dream.*

    * In a lovely garden walking,
      Two lovers went hand in hand;
    Two wan, worn figures, talking
      They sat in the flowery land.

    On the cheek they kissed one another,
      On the mouth so sweetly fain :
    Fast holding each the other,
      They were young and well again.

    Two little bells rang shrilly—
      The dream went with the hour :
    She lay in the cloister stilly,
      He far in the dungeon-tower!
                From Uhland.

Hanging his head, behind each came a hound,
Padding with gentle paws upon the road.
Straight silent pines rose here and there around ;
A dull stream on the left side hardly flowed ;
A black snake through the sluggish waters wound.
Hark, the night-raven ! see the crawling toad !
She thinks how dark will be the moonless night ;
For feeblest ray is yet supernal light.

The moon's last gleam fell on dim glazed eyes :
His body shrunken from his garments' fold,
Stooping with bended knees that could not rise,
An old man tottered in the maiden's hold.
She shuddered—though too slender the disguise
To hide from love what never yet was old !
She held him closer, closed her eyes to pray,
Walked through the fear, and kept the onward way.

Towards a gloomy thicket of tall firs,
Dragging his inch-long steps, he turned aside.
Silent it was—no driest needle stirs.
They enter—and a breeze begins to chide
In the cone-tops. It swells until it whirs
Through bare thin stems and branches tufted wide—
The rooted grove a harp of mighty chords,
Wing-smote by viewless creatures wild for words.

But when he turned again, towards the cleft
Of a huge hollow rock, it instant ceased;
And the tall pines stood sudden—as if reft
Of a strong passion, or from pain released;
Again they wove their strange, dark, moveless weft
Across the midnight sky; and west and east
Cloud-giants rose and marched up cloudy stairs;
And like sad thoughts the bats came unawares.

'Twas a drear chamber for thy bridal night,
O poor, pale, saviour bride ! An earthen lamp
With shaking hands he kindled, whose faint light
Mooned out a tiny halo on the damp
That filled the cavern to its unseen height—
Shining like dim death-candle on a swamp,
Watching the entrance, each side lies a hound —
With liquid light his green eyes gleaming round.

A heap rose grave-like from the rocky floor,
Of moss and leaves, by many a sunny wind
Long tossed and dried—with rich furs covered o'er,
Expectant. Up a jealous glory shined
In her lone heart!—he had expected more
From her than from those faithless ! With sweet
    mind,
She praying gently did herself unclothe,
And lay beside him, trusting, and not loath.

Once more the wind among the trees o'erhead!
The hounds pricked up their ears, their eyes
    flashed fire.
The trembling maiden heard a sodden tread—
Dull, yet importunate through the tempest's ire,
As if long dripping feet o'er smooth stones sped —
Come fiercely up, as with a longing dire
To enter. Followed sounds of hurried rout.
With bristling hair, the hounds stood looking
    out.

Then came, half querulous, a whisper old,
Feeble and hollow as if shut in a chest:
"Take my face on your bosom: I am cold."
She bared her holy bosom's truth-white nest,
And forth her two hands instant went, love-bold,
And took the face, and close against her pressed.
Ah, the dead chill! and—could it be the rain?—
But one great heart kept beating for the twain.

She heard the wind fall, and the following rain,
And then a water growing, till the sound
Went roaring through the night across the plain.
The lamp went out, by the slow darkness drowned.—
Must the fair dawn for ages long refrain?
Like centuries the feeble hours went round.
Eternal night entombed her with decay,
To her live bosom clasping breathless clay.

The world stood still. Her life sunk down so low,
That but for wretchedness, no life she knew.
A charnel wind moaned out a moaning—*No;*
From the sepulchral heart of earth it blew.
Fair memories had lost their sunset glow.
Out of the dark the forms of old friends grew,
But so transparent blanched with dole and smart,
She saw the pale worm lying in each heart.

And worst of all—O death of keep-fled life!
A voice within her woke and cried: In sooth,
Vain is all sorrow, hope, and care, and strife;
Yea, love and beauty, tenderness and truth,
Are shadows bred in hearts too fancy-rife,
And pass and die with sure-decaying youth:
Give them a glance, they quiver, waver, blot;
Gaze at them fixedly, and they are not.

And all the answer the poor child could make
Was the close tightened grasp of her two hands.
Alone she lay, slow mouldering, awake
Within the strong grave's unrelaxing bands,
And death alone was good—but for his sake.
The darksome horror grew like drifting sands,
Till nought was precious — neither God, nor
    light;
And yet she braved the false, denying night.

So dead was hope, that when a glimmer weak
Stole through some crevice in the rocky wall,
And thinned the clotted darkness on his cheek,
She thought she lay to some poor dream in thrall.
But back he drew his head, her face to seek,
And gaze with eyes that asked yet knew it all:
Old age, convicted lie, had fled away,
And youth eternal in her bosom lay!

With a low cry closer to him she crept,
And on his bosom hid a face that glowed:
It was his turn to comfort—he had slept.
She had been faithful: outworn with the load
Of dark endurance, long-pent love she wept.
A sunny rain their tears, joy-smitten, flowed
Fit baptism for new life from darkness won.
Weeping they slept, and waited for the sun.

THE LOST SOUL.

Send your eyes across the gray,
By my finger-point away,
Through the fumy, thickened air.
Beyond the air, you see the dark;
Beyond the dark, the dawning day:
On its horizon, pray you, mark
Something like a ruined heap
Of worlds half-uncreated, that go back
Slow to the awful deep
Of nothingness, bare being's lack,
Down all the stairs whereby they rose
Up to harmonious life, and law's repose:
On its surface, lone and bare,

THE LOST SOUL.

Shapeless as a dumb despair,
Formless, nameless, something lies :
Can the vision in your eyes
Its idea recognize ?

 A poor lost soul it is, alack !—
Half he lived some ages back.
But, with half-way opened eyes,
Thinking him already wise,
Down he sat and wrote a book—
Drew his life into a nook,
And out of it would not arise
To read the letters dim,
The sayings dark upon his walls ;
He said they were but chance-led scrawls,
Or at the best no use to him.
He had a lamp for reading these—
He trimmed it as he sat at ease,
Sat at ease and would not look—

Trimmed it down to one faint spark :
It went out, and left him dark.
Let me try if he will hear
Spirit words with spirit ear.

Motionless thing ! who once
Like him who cries to thee,
Hadst thy place in the mystic dance
From the doors of the far eternity, —
A place in the dance of thy radiant peers,
Issuing ever, with feet that glance
To the joyous law that binds the free,
To the clang of the crystal spheres !
O heart for love ! O thirst to drink
From the wells that feed the sea !
O hands of truth — a golden link
'Twixt mine and the Father's knee !
O eyes to see ! O soul to think !

THE LOST SOUL.

O life, the brother of me !
Has the Infinite sucked back all
The individual life it gave?
Boots it nothing to cry and call?
Is thy form an empty grave?

It heareth not, brothers — we need not tarry !
Sounds no sense to its ear will carry ;
Sting it with words, it will never shrink :
It cannot repent, it will not think.
Hath God forgotten it, alas !
Lost in eternity's lumber room ?
Will the wind of his breathing never pass
Over it through the insensate gloom ?
Like a frost-killed bud on a tombstone curled,
Crumbling it lies on its crumbling world.
Sightless and soundless, with never a cry,
In the hell of its own vacuity !

See, see yon angel cross our flight,
Where the thunder vapours loom—
From his upcast pinions flashing the light
Of some outbreaking doom!
—Up, brothers! away! a storm is nigh!
Smite we the wing up a steeper sky!
What matters the hail or the clashing winds—
The thunder that buffets, the lightning that blinds?
We know by the tempest we do not lie
Dead in the pits of eternity!

THE THREE HORSES.

WHAT shall I be?—I will be a knight
   Walled up in armour black,
With a sword of sharpness, a hammer of might,
   And a spear that will not crack—
So black, so blank, no glimmer of light
   Shall betray my darkling track.

Saddle my coal-black steed, my men,
   Fittest for sunless work;
Old Night is steaming from her den,
   Her children gather and lurk;
Bad things are creeping from the fen,
   And sliding down the murk.

Let him go!—let him go! Let him plunge!—
    Keep away!
  He's a foal of the third seal's brood!
Gaunt with armour, in full array
    Of poitrel and frontlet-hood,
Let him go—with clang and clatter away,
    Right for the evil wood.

I and Ravenwing on the course—
    Heavy in fighting gear—
Woe to the thing that checks our force,
    That meets us in career!
Giant, enchanter, devil, or worse—
    Have at him with couched spear!

Through the trees clanking I ride.
    See—the goblins—to and fro!
From the skull of the darkness, deep and wide,
    The eyes of dragons glow.

From the thickets the silent serpents glide.
　But I pass—I let them go.

For I shall find in the evil night
　Some little one crying alone;
Some aged knight, outworn in fight,
　And by caitiffs stricken prone;
Or a lady with terror staring white,
　And her senses almost flown.

The child in my arms to my hauberk prest,
　Like a trembling bird I feel;
I cover him round, as in a nest,
　With sheltering wings of steel,
And bear him home to his mother's breast.
　And the lips that soothe and heal.

Or, spur in flank, and lance in rest,
　On the ol knight's foes I flash;

The knaves I scatter to east and west,
   With clang and hurtle and crash;
And leave them the law, as such learn it best
   In bruise, and breach, and gash.

Or, the lady I lift on my panting steed,
   And with spear for staff I stalk;
With hand on bridle gently lead
   The horse in a careful walk;
With keen-shot glance the thickets heed,
   And only in whispers talk.

For evil is round us, and forest, and night,
   Where glow the dragons' eyes,
Where wander lawless men of might,
   And from clefts the goblins rise!—
I *will* be a knight that loves the right,
   And mounts for it till he dies.

Alas! 'tis a dream of ages hoar!
   In the fens no dragons blow;
Fell giants no ladies fair implore;
   Through the forest wide roadways go:
If I loved as loved the knights of yore,
   Where is the deed to show?

If I should saddle old Ravenwing,
   And hie me out at night,
The little scared birds away would spring,
   An ill-shot arrow's flight.—
The idle fancy away I fling,
   And now I will dream aright.

Bridle me Twilight, my dapple-gray,
   With broad rein and snaffle bit.
Let a youth bring him round to the door, I say,
   When the shadows begin to flit—

Just as the darkness is dreaming away,
   And the owls begin to sit.

Unarmed of mail or shield, I go,
   With just my sword—gray-blue
Like the scythe of the morning, come to mow
   The night-sprung shadows anew
From the paths of the east, that, fair and slow,
   Maid morning may walk through.

I seek no forest with darkness grim—
   To the open land I ride,
As the dawn from the broad horizon's brim
   Lies wet on the flowing tide,
And mottles with shadows dun and dim
   The mountain's rugged side.

Our way lies over dale and hill,
   Over moor and beach;

Nor bridle I draw, nor slacken, until
    Some city of men we reach ;
There, in the market, he stands still,
    And I lift my voice and preach.

Wealth and poverty, age and youth
    Around me gather and throng;
And I tell them of justice, of wisdom, of truth,
    Of righteousness, law, and wrong,
Till my words are moulded by right and ruth
    To a solemn-chanted song.

And they bring me questions which would be scanned,
    That strife may be forgot ;
Swerves my balance to neither hand ;
    The poor I favour no jot :
If a man withstand, outsweeps my brand—
    I wipe away the blot.

But what if the eye has in it a beam,
   That spies in his the mote?
Righteousness only, and wisdom supreme,
   Can tell the sheep from the goat!
This is not the dream that I may dream—
   Not the law that I may quote.

Turn Twilight back. I dare not kill.
   The sword myself would scare,—
When the sun looks over the eastern hill,
   Bring out my snow-white mare:
One labour is left which no one will
   Deny me the right to share.

Take heed, my men, from crest to heel
   Snow-white have no speck.
No curb, no bit her mouth must feel,
   No tightening rein her neck;

No saddle-girth, with buckles of steel
   Her mighty breathing check.

Lay on her a cloth of silver sheen;
   Bring me a robe of white;
For wherever we go, we must be seen
   By the shining of our light—
A glistening splendour in forest green,
   A star on the mountain-height.

With a jar and a shudder the gates unclose—
   Out in the sun she leaps!
A unit of light and power she goes,
   Levelling plains and steeps;
The wind around her eddies and blows,
   Behind and before her sleeps.

Oh joy, oh joy to ride the world
   And holy tidings bear!

The white flag of peace on the winds unfurled
   Is the mane of my shining mare:
From heaven to hell see Satan hurled
   Like lightning through the air!

Oh, the sun and the wind! Oh, the life and the
   love!
   Where the serpent swung all day,
The loud dove coos to the silent dove;
   Where the web-winged dragon lay,
In its hole beneath, on its rock above,
   Merry-tongued children play.

With eyes of light the maidens look up,
   As they weave their garlands sweet,
From lapfuls of green blade and golden cup,
   For the infants about their feet:
I call my message—I must not stop
   My oldest friend to greet.

For the message itself is might and mirth
   To city and land of corn—
Praise for heaviness, plenty for dearth,
   For darkness a dawning morn:
Clap hands, ye billows, be glad, O earth—
   For a child, a child is born!

Now, even the just shall live by faith,
   Nor argue of mine and thine;
Old self shall die an ecstatic death,
   And be born a thing divine,
For God's own being and God's own breath
   Shall be its bread and wine.

Ambition shall vanish, and Love be king,
   And Pride to his darkness hie;
Yea, for very love of a living thing
   A man would forget and die,

If very love were not the spring
   That life goes living by.

The myrtle shall spring where grew the thorn;
   Earth shall be young as heaven;
The heart with remorse or anger torn,
   Shall weep like a summer even;
For to us a child, a child is born,
   Unto us a son is given!

Ah!—Holy message!—I dare not ride!
   I am a fool—a beast!—
Where kings for service in vain have sighed,
   I anoint myself a priest!—
With worst ambition—to sit beside
   The master of the feast!

Lead Snow-white back to her glimmering stall:
   There let her stand and feed.

I am overweening, ignorant, small.—
  Yet, Lord—I will take good heed—
Let me wash the hoofs and be the thrall
  Of the shining gospel-steed.

THE GOLDEN KEY.

In haste to pass, the vapours curled—
   The sun was in the air;
The boy awoke—and lo, the world
   Was waiting for him there!

The fields, the waters, all the earth
   Was full of windy play—
Shining and fair and full of mirth,
   All for his holiday.

The hill said "Climb me;" and the wood—
   "Come to my bosom, child;
I have a merry gamboling brood,
   But thou art far more wild."

The shadows with the sunlight played,
    The birds were singing loud;
The hill stood up with pines arrayed,
    And not a single cloud.

But long ere noon, dark grew the skies,
    And pale the shrinking sun.
"How soon," he said, "for clouds to rise,
    When day was but begun!"

The wind grew wild. A wilful power,
    It swept o'er tree and town.
The boy exulted for an hour,
    Then weary sat him down.

And as he sat the rain began,
    And rained till all was still:
He looked, and saw a rainbow span
    The vale from hill to hill.

He dried his tears. "Ah! now," he said,
  "The storm was good, I see:
Yon shining hill—upon its head
  I'll find the golden key."

He thrid the copse, he climbed the fence,
  At last the top did scale;—
When, lo! the rainbow, vanished thence,
  Was shining in the vale!

"But here it stood.—Yes, here," he said,
  "Its very foot was set;
I saw this fir-tree through the red,
  This through the violet."

He searched and searched, while down the skies
  Went slow the slanting sun.
At length he lifted hopeless eyes,
  And day was nearly done.

Beyond the vale, beyond the heath,
　　Low flamed the crimson west;
His mother's cottage lay beneath,
　　In rosy radiance drest.

"Oh joy!" he cried—"not *all* the way
　　Farther from home we go!
The rain will come another day,
　　And bring another bow."

But ere he reached his mother's cot,
　　Weary, with rest before,
The red was all one cold gray blot,
　　And night lay round the door.

But when his mother stroked his head,
　　The night was grim in vain;
And when she kissed him in his bed,
　　The rainbow rose again.

Soon, things that are and things that seem
   Did mingle merrily;
He dreamed — nor was it all a dream —
   His mother had the key.

SOMNIUM MYSTICI.

A MICROCOSM IN TERZA RIMA.

I.

QUIET I lay at last, and knew no more
   Whether I breathed or not—so worn I lay
   With the death-struggle. What was yet before
Neither I met, nor turned from it away.
   My only conscious being was the deep rest
   Of torture dead—gone with the bygone day.
And long I could have lingered—all but blest,
   In that slow dreamy pause. But came a sound
   As of a door that opened – in the west
Somewhere I thought it was. The noise unbound
   The sleep from off my eyelids, and they rose,

And I looked forth. And looking, straight I
    found
It was my chamber-door that did unclose,
    Whence a tall form up to my bedside drew—
    Grand, silent, bending almost with repose;
And when I saw his countenance, I knew
    That I was lying in my chamber dead;
    For this my brother—brothers such are few—
That now to greet me bowed his kingly head,
    Had, many years agone, like holy dove
    Returning, from his friends and kindred sped,
And, leaving memories of mournful love,
    Passed vanishing behind the unseen veil;
    And though I loved him, all high words above.
Not for his loss then did I weep or wail,
    Knowing that here we live but in a tent,
    And that our house is yonder, without fail:
Now eager, up to meet him, slow I bent—
    I too was dead, so might the dead embrace.

The dear, long-fingered hand silent he lent,
And lifted me. I was in feeble case,
  But growing stronger, stood upon the floor;
  Then turned and once regarded my dead face,
With curious eyes: its brow contentment bore —
  But I had done with it. I turned away,
  And seeing my brother by the open door,
Followed him out into the night blue-gray.
  The houses stood up hard in limpid air,
  The moon hung in the heavens in half decay,
And all the world to my bare feet lay bare.

. . .

II.

Now I had suffered in my life — as they
  Suffer who still by slow years younger grow,
  And feel the false vain self dropping away,
Which, born of greed and fear, had gathered
    slow,

Darkening the angel-self that, evermore,
  Where no vain phantom in or out shall go,
Moveless beholds the Father—stands before
  The throne of revelation, waiting there,
  With wings low-drooping on the sapphire-
      floor,
Until they find the Father's ideal fair,
  And are themselves at last: not one small
      thorn
  Shall needless any pilgrim's garments tear;
And thus to speak of suffering I would scorn,
  But for a marvellous thing that next befell:—
  Sudden I grew aware I was new-born;
All pain had vanished in the absorbing swell
  Of some exalting peace that was my own:
  As the moon dwelt in heaven, did calmness
      dwell
At home in me, essential. The earth's moan
  Lay all behind. Had I then lost my part

SOMNIUM MYSTICI.

In human griefs—dear part with them that
    groan?
"'Tis weariness," I said; but with a start
    That set it trembling, and yet brake it not.
    I found the peace was love. Oh, my rich
        heart!—
For every time I caught a glimmering spot
    Of window pane -- "There, in that silent
        room,"
    I thought, "sleeps one in whose expanding lot
I have a part:"—I cared for that one, whom
    I saw not, had not seen, and might not see.
    After the love crept prone its shadow-gloom;
But instant a mightier love arose in me—
    As in an ocean a single wave might swell—
    And heaved the shadow to the centre: we
Had called it prayer. before on sleep I fell.
    It sank, and left my sea in holy calm:
    I gave each man to God, and all was well.

On my left side my brother, with one palm
  Stretched open out, level before him, went
  One step in front of me.   A heavenly balm
Flowed from his presence—ere long with sadness
    blent.

III.

Nor softest murmur through the city crept,
  Nor one lone word my brother to me had spoken;
  But when beyond the city-gate we stept,
I knew the silent spell would soon be broken.
    A cool night wind came whispering : through
        and through
    It soft baptized me with the pledge and token
Of that sweet spirit-wind which blows and blew,
  And fans the human world since evermore.
  The very grass, cool to my feet, I knew
To be love also, and with the love I bore

To hold far sympathy, silent and sweet,
   As having known the secret from of yore.
And now my heart was eager all to meet
   The eyes and voice of him who onward led,
   When he stood sudden, and, with arrested feet,
I also. Like a half-sunned orb, his head
   Slow turned the bright side: Lord, the brother-
       smile
That ancient human glory on me shed,
In which thou clothed camest forth to wile
   Unto thy bosom every labouring soul,
   And its dividing passions to beguile
To a glad winsome death, and on them roll
   The blessed stone of the Holy Sepulchre.
   "Brother," he said, "thou art like me now—
       whole
And sound and well; for the keen pain, and stir
   Uneasy, and the grief that came to us all,
   In that we knew not how the wine and myrrh

Could ever from the vinegar and gall
    Be parted—are deep sunk, yea drowned in God;
    And yet the past not folded in a pall,
But breathed upon, like Aaron's withered rod,
    By a sweet light that brings the blossoms through—
    Showing in dreariest paths that men have trod,
Another's foot-prints, spotted of crimson hue,
    Still on before, wherever theirs did wend;
    Yea, through the desert leading—of thyme and
        rue,
The desert souls in which the lions rend
    And roar—the passionate who, to be blest,
    Ravin as bears, and do not gain their end,
Because that, save in God, can be no rest."

IV.

Something my brother said to me like this—
    But how unlike it also, think, I pray:

His eyes were music, and his smile a kiss ;
Himself the word, his speech was but a ray
   In the clear nimbus that with verity
   Of absolute utterance made a home-born day
Of truth about him, lamping solemnly.
   And when he paused, there came a swift repose,
   Too high, too still to be called ecstasy—
A purple silence, lanced through in the close
   By such keen thought, it grew, suddenly smiling,
   Sheen silver with a heart of burning rose.
It was a glory full of reconciling,
   Of perfect faithfulness, and love, and pain ;
   Of tenderness, and care, and mother-wiling
Back to the bosom of a speechless gain.

V.

I cannot tell how long we joyous talked,
    For from my sense old time had vanished
        quite,
    Space dim remaining—for onward still we
        walked.
No sun arose to blot the pale, still night—
    Still as the night of some great spongy stone
    That turns but once an age betwixt the light
And the huge shadow from its own bulk
        thrown ;—
    Long as that night to me—before whose face
    Visions so many slid, and veils were blown
Aside from the vague vast of Isis' grace.
    Innumerous thoughts did throng that infinite
        hour,
    And in me hopes did hopes unceasing chase,
For I was all responsive to his power.

I saw my friends weep, wept, and let them
    weep:
I saw the dawn of the grief-nurtured flower,
And the gardener Jesus watching—in their sleep
    Wiping their tears with the napkin he had laid
    Wrapped by itself when he climbed Hades
    steep.
Faith found it easy there; but undismayed
    I also saw the abortive monsters nursed
    In slimy coverts—the rich man that preyed,
And the poor man that ground his neighbour
    worst;
    Yea all the human chaos, wild and waste,
    Where what high God for evermore hath cursed,
To madder wallowing is stung and chased
    By dim recallings of the good forgot.
    But he that will believe shall not make haste;
For God may shut into a seed no jot
    Less than an aeon; give a world that lay

Wombed in its sun, a molten unorbed clot,
One moment from the red rim to spin away,
   Librating — ages to roll on weary wheel,
   Ere home it come — fulfilled its year-full day:
Who in the chiliad sees the day, shall feel
   No anxious heart, shall lift no trembling hand;
   But, keen-dividing as the sword of steel
That from His mouth went forth in Patmos-land,
   Shall ever hope, and, to his labour bent,
   The Father's will shall, doing, understand.
So spake my brother as we onward went:
   I drank his words, as dew the summer-lea,
   Till faith had almost blossomed in content.
We came at last upon a lonesome sea.

IV.

Right onward still he went, I following
    Out on the water. But the water, lo!
    Like a thin sheet of glass, lay vanishing;
The starry host in glorious two-fold show
    Shone up, shone down! and soon as I saw this
    A quivering dread thorough my heart did go:
Unstayed, I walked athwart a twin abyss,
    A hollow sphere of blue! nor floor was found
    Of seeing eye, only the foot met the kiss
Of the cool water, lightly crisping round
    The edges of the footsteps! Terror froze
    My fallen eyelids. But again the sound
Of my guide's voice on the still air arose.
    " Hast thou forgotten that we walk by faith?
    For keenest sight but multiplies the shows.
Lift up thine eyelids; take a valiant breath;

Fearful, dare yet the terror in God's name;
Step wider; trust the invisible. Can Death
Avail no more to hearten up thy flame?"
I trembled, but I opened wide mine eyes,
And strode on the invisible sea. The same
High moment vanished all my cowardice,
And God was with me; the well-pleased stars
Threw quivering smiles across the guily skies,
And the aurora flashed great scimitars
    From north to zenith; and once more my
        guide
Full turned with blessed face. No prison-bars
Latticed across a soul I there descried,
No weather-stains of grief; quiet age-long
Brooded upon his forehead clear and wide;
Yet from that face a pang shot; vivid and
        strong.
Into my heart; for though I saw him stand
Close to me in the void as one in a throng,

Yet on the border of some nameless land
  He stood afar; a still-eyed mystery
  Caught him whole worlds away. Though in
    my hand
His hand I held, and gazing earnestly,
  Searched in his countenance, as in a mine,
  For jewels of contentment, satisfy
My heart I could not. Seeming to divine
  My hidden trouble, gently he stooped and
    kissed
  My forehead, and his arms did round me twine,
And held me to his bosom. Still I missed
  That ancient earthly nearness, when we shared
  One bed, like birds that of no morrow wist;
Roamed our one father's farm; or, later, fared
  Along the dusty highways of the old clime.
  Backward he drew, and, as if having bared
My soul, stood reading there a little time;
  And in his eyes tears gathered slow, like dew

That dims the grass at evening or at prime,
But makes the stars clear-goldener in the blue;
   And on his lips a faint ethereal smile
   Hovered, as hangs the mist of its own hue
Trembling about a purple flower, the while
   Evening grows brown. "Brother! brother!"
      I cried;
But straight outbursting tears my words beguile,
And in my bosom all the utterance died.

VII.

A moment more he stood, and softly sighed.—
   "I know thy pain; but this sorrow is far
   Beyond my help," at length his voice replied
To my beseeching tears. "Look at yon star
   Up from the low east half-way—all ablaze:
   Think'st thou, because no cloud between doth
      mar

The liquid glory that from its visage rays,
  Thou therefore knowest that same world on
    high,
  Its people and its orders and its ways?"
"What meanest thou?" I said. "Thou know'st
    that I
  Would hold, not thy dear form, but the self-
    thee.
  Thou art not near me. For thyself I cry."
"Not the less near that nearer I shall be.
  I have a world within thou dost not know:
    Would I could make thee know it! But all of
    me
Is thine; though thou not yet canst enter so
  Into possession, that betwixt us twain
  The frolic homeliness of love should flow
As o'er the brim of childhood's cup again:
  Away the deeper childhood first must wipe
  That clouded consciousness which was our pain.

When in thy breast the godlike hath grown ripe,
    And thou, Christ's little one, art ten times more
    A child than when we played with drum and pipe
About our earthly father's happy door,
    Then—" He ceased not; his holy utterance still
    Flowing went on like spring from hidden store
Of wasteless waters; but I wept my fill,
    Nor heeded much the comfort of his speech.
    At length he said: "When first I clomb the hill—
With earthly words I heavenly things would reach—
    Where dwelleth now the man we used to call
    Father, whose voice—oh memory dear!—did teach
Us in our beds, and straight, as once a stall
    A temple, holy grew the sportful room—
    Prone on the ground before him I did fall,
So grand he towered above me like a doom;

But now I look into the well-known face
Fearless, yea, basking blessed in the bloom
Of his eternal youthfulness and grace."
"But something separates us," yet I cried;
"Let light at least begin the dark to chase,
The dark begin to waver and divide,
And clear the path of vision. In the old time,
When clouds one heart did from the other hide,
A wind would blow between. If one would climb,
This foot must rise ere that can go up higher:
Some big A teach me of the eternal prime."—
He answered then: "Hearts that to love aspire,
Must learn its mighty harmony ere they can
Falter one perfect note in its great quire.
Yet thereto am I sent—oh, sent of one
Who makes the dumb for joy break out and sing
He opens every door 'twixt man and man;
He to the inner chamber all will bring."

VIII.

It was enough: hope waked from dreary swound,
  And hope had ever been enough for me—
  To kennel driving grim to-morrow's hound,
From chains of school and custom setting free,
  Had urged my life to living.—On we went,
  Across the stars that underlay the sea,
And came to a blown shore of sand and bent.
  Beyond the sand a marshy moor we crossed,
  Silent—I, for I pondered what he meant,
And he, that sacred speech might not be lost.
  At length we came upon an evil place.
  Trees lay about like a half-buried host,
Each in its desolate pool. Some fearful race
  Of creatures was not far, for howls and cries
  And gurgling hisses came. With even pace
Walking, " Fear not," he said, " for this way lies

Our journey." On we went; and soon the ground
Slow from the waste began a gentle rise ;
And tender grass, here, there, now all around,
Came clouding up with its fresh homely tinge
Of softest green cold-flushing every mound ;
At length, of lowly shrubs a scattered fringe.

IX.

And last, a wildered forest, somewhat blind,
With a brown shadowless light ; nor, all the year,
Part once its branches in a blowing wind ;
So still, its trees, unwithering, appear
To ponder on the past, as men may do
That for the future wait without a fear.
I know not if for days many or few
Pathless we thrid the wood ; for never sun,

At sylvan-traceried windows peeping through,
Mottled with brighter green the mosses dun,
  Or meted with moving shadows Time, the
    shade.
  No life was there—not even a spider spun.
At length we came into a sky-roofed glade,
  An open level, in a circle shut
  By solemn trees that stood aside and made
Large room and lonely for a little hut,
  By grassy sweeps wide-margined from the wood.
  'Twas built of saplings old, that had been cut
When those great trees no larger by them stood,
  And, thick with ancient moss, it seemed to have
    grown
  Thus from the old brown earth, a covert rude,
Half-house, half-grave, half-lifted up, half-prone.
  Up to its door my brother led me. "There
  Is thy low school," he said; "there be thou
    shown

 Thy pictured alphabet. Wake a mind of prayer,
  And praying enter." "But wilt thou not come,
  Brother?" I said. "No," said he. And I—
   "Where
Then shall I find thee? Thou wilt not leave me
   dumb,
  And a whole world of thoughts unuttered?"
  With half-sad smile, and dewy eyes, and some
Conflicting motions of his kingly head,
  He pointed to the open-standing door.
  I entered: inward, lo, my shadow led!
I turned—his countenance shone like lightning
   hoar!
  But slow he turned from me, and parted slow,
  Like one unwilling, whom I should see no more;
With voice nor hand, said *Farewell! I must go,*
  But drew the clinging door hard to the post.
  No dry leaves rustled 'neath his going; no
Footfalls came back from the departing ghost.

He was no more. I laid me down and wept.
Nor dared to follow him—restrained the most
By fear I should not see him if I swept
Out after him on wings of pleading love.
Close to the wall, in hopeless loss, I crept.
There cool sleep came, God's shadow, from above.

X.

I woke, with calmness cleansed and sanctified—
The peace that filled my heart of old, when I
Woke in my mother's lap; for since I died,
The past lay bare, even to the dreaming shy
That shadowed my yet gathering unborn brain.
And, marvelling, on the floor I saw, close by
My elbow-pillowed head, as if it had lain
Beside me all the time I dreamless lay,
A little pool of sunlight, which did stain
The earthen brown with gold; marvelling, I say,

Because across the sea and through the wood
　No sun had shone upon me all the way.
I rose, and through a chink the glade I viewed,
　But all was dull as it before had been,
　And sunless every tree-top round it stood,
With hardly light enough to show it green;
　Yet through the broken roof, serenely glad,
　By a rough hole entered that heavenly sheen.
Then I remembered in old years I had
　Seen such a light—where, with dropt eyelids
　　　gloomed
　Upon an earthen floor dark women sad—
In a low barn-like house, where lay entombed
　Their sires and children; only there the door
　Was open to the sun, which entering plumed
With shadowy palms the stones that filled the floor,
　Set up like lidless chests—and so did find
　That memory needs no brain, but keeps her store
In hidden chambers of the eternal mind.

Thence backward ran the roused memory
Down the ever-opening vista—back to blind
Anticipations, while my soul did lie
    Closed in my mother's; forward thence through
        bright
    Spring morns of childhood, gay with hopes that
        fly
Bird-like across their doming blue and white;
    Through passionate summer noons, down to sad
        eves
    Of autumn rain, and on to wintered night;
Thence up once more to dewy dawn, that weaves
    Saffron and gold— weaves hope with still con-
        tent,
    And wakes the worship that even wrong bereaves
Of half its pain. And round her as she went,
    Hovered a sense as of an odour dear
    Whose flower was far—as of a letter sent,
Not yet arrived—a footstep coming near,

But oh, how long delayed the lifting latch !—
As of a waiting sun, ready to peer,
Yet peering not—as of a breathless watch
Over a sleeping beauty—babbling rhyme
About her lips, but no winged word to catch !
And here I lay—the child of changeful time
Shut in the weary, changeless evermore,
A dull, eternal, fadeless autumn clime !
Was this the dungeon of my sinning sore—
A gentle hell of loneliness, foredoomed
For such as I, whose love was yet the core
Of all my being ? The brown shadow gloomed
Persistent, faded, warm. No ripple ran
Across the air, no roaming insect boomed.
"Alas !" I cried, "I am no living man !
Better were darkness and the leave to grope,
Than light that builds its own drear prison ! Can
This be the folding of the wings of hope ?"

XI.

That instant, through the branches overhead
   Sounds of a going went. A shadow fell
   Prone in the unrippled pool of sunlight fed
From some far fountain hid in heavenly dell.
   I looked, and in the low roof's broken place
   A single snowdrop stood—a radiant bell
Of silvery shine, softly subdued by grace
   Of delicate green, that made the white appear
   Yet whiter. Blind it bowed its head a space,
Half-timid—then, as in despite of fear,
   It spread its three white rays. If it had swung
   Its pendent bell, and music golden clear—
Division just entrancing sounds among—
   Had flickered down as tender as flakes of snow,
   It had not shed more influence as it rung
Than from its look alone did rain and flow.
   I knew the flower; saw to its human ways;

Dim saw the secret that had made it grow:
My heart supplied the music's golden phrase.
   Light from the dark and snowdrops from the
      earth—
   Life's resurrection out of gross decays—
The endless round of beauty's yearly birth—
   And nations' rise and fall—were in the flower,
   And read themselves in silence. Heavenly mirth
Awoke in my sad heart. For one whole hour
   I praised the God of snowdrops. But at height
   The bliss gave way. Next faith began to cower.
And then the snowdrop vanished from my sight.

XII.

Last, I began in unbelief to say:
   "No angel this! a snowdrop—nothing more!
   A trifle which God's hands drew forth in play

From the tangled pond of Chaos, dark and frore,
    And threw on the bank and left blindly to breed!
    A wilful fancy would have gathered store
Of evanescence from the pretty weed—
    White, pendent—so divine!—conclusion lame,
    O'erdriven into the shelter of a creed!
Not out of God but nothingness it came:
    Colourless, feeble, flying from life's heat,
    It has no honour, hardly shunning shame—"
When—see! another shadow at my feet!
    Hopeless I lifted now my weary head:
    Lo, at my window another heavenly cheat!—
A primrose fair, from its rough-blanketed bed
    Laughing my unbelief to heavenly scorn—
    A sun-child, just awake, no prayer yet said,
Half-rising from the couch where it was born,
    And smiling to the heavens! I breathed again;
    Out of the midnight once more dawned the morn!
And fled the phantom doubt, with all its train!

XII.

I was a child once more, nor measured life,
    Nor thought of what or how much. All my soul
With sudden births of lovely things grew rife.
A daisy at heaven's window? Instant roll
    Rich lawny fields, with red tips crowding the green,
Across the hollows, over ridge and knoll,
To where the rosy sun goes down serene.
    In at the window peers a pimpernel?
    I walked in morning scents of thyme and bean
Dew-drops on every stalk and bud and bell
    Flashed, like a jewel-orchard, many roods;
    Glowed ruby suns, which emerald suns would quell:
Topaz saint-glories, sapphire beatitudes,
    Blazed in the slanting sunshine all around;

Above, the high priest lark, o'er fields and
    woods—
Rich-hearted with his five eggs on the ground—
    The sacrifice bore through the veil of light,
    Odour and colour offering up in sound.—
Filled heart-full thus with forms of lowly might
    And shapeful silences of lovely lore,
    I sat a child, happy with only sight;
And for a time I needed nothing more.

XVI.

Prone to the revelation I did lie—
    Passive as prophet to his dreaming deep,
    Or harp Æolian to the breathing sky;
And blest as any child whom twilight sleep
    Holds half, and half lets go. But the new day
    Of higher need up-dawned with sudden leap:
"Ah, flowers," I said, "ye are divinely gay!

But your fair music is too far and fine;
Ye are full cups, yet reach not to allay
The drought of those for human love who pine,
As harts for water-brooks." At once a face
Was looking in my face; its eyes through mine
Were feeding me with tenderness and grace;
And by their love I knew my mother's eyes.
And as I gazed there grew in me apace
A longing grief; and love did swell and rise,
Till weeping I brake out and did bemoan
My blameful share in bygone tears and cries.
"O mother, wilt thou plead for me?" I groan;
"I say not, plead with Christ—but plead with those
Who, gathered now in peace about his throne,
Were near me when my heart was full of throes,
And longings vain after a flying bliss,
Which oft the fountain by the threshold froze:
They must forgive me—mother. Tell them this.

No more shall swell the love-dividing sigh:
Down at their feet I lay my selfishness."
The face grew passionate at this my cry;
The gathering tears up to its eyebrims rose;
It grew a trembling mist, that did not fly,
But slow dissolved. I wept as one of those
Who wake outside the garden of their dream,
And lo, the droop-winged hours laborious close
Its opal gates with stone and stake and beam!

XV.

But glory went that glory more might come.
Behold a countless multitude—no less!
A host of faces, me besieging, dumb
In the lone castle of my mournfulness!
Had then my mother given the word I sent,
And gathered those out of the shining press?
And had these others their love aidance lent

For full assurance of the pardon prayed?
Would they concentre love, with sweet intent,
On my self-love, to blast the evil shade?
Ah, perfect vision! pledge of endless hope!
Oh army of the Holy Spirit, arrayed
In comfort's panoply! For words I grope—
For clouds to catch your radiant dawn, my own,
And tell your coming! From the highest cope
Of blue, down to my windows came a cone
Of faces and their eyes—O loveliest morn!—
Bright heads down-bending like the forward blown,
Heavy with ripeness, golden ears of corn,
By gentle wind on crowded harvest-field—
All bending to my prison-hut forlorn,
As if with power of eyes they would have healed
My troubled heart—making it like their own,
In which the bitter fountain had been sealed,
And the life-giving water flowed alone!

XVI.

With what I thus beheld, glorified then—
  "God, let me love my fill and pass!" I sighed,
  And dead, for love had almost died again.
"O fathers, brothers, I am yours!" I cried;
  "O mothers, sisters, I am nothing now
  Save as I am yours, and in you sanctified!
O men, O women, of the peaceful brow,
  And infinite abysses in the eyes,
  Whence God's ineffable gazes on me! how
Care ye for me, impassioned and unwise?
  Oh ever draw my heart out after you!
  Ever, O grandeur, thus before me rise.
And I need nothing!—not even for love will sue!
  I am no more, and love is all in all.
  Henceforth there is, there can be nothing new—
All things are always new." Then, like the fall
  Of a steep avalanche, my joy fell steep:

Up in my spirit rose as it were the call
Of an old sorrow from an ancient deep;
  For when my eyes fixed on the eyes of him
  Whom I had loved before I learned to creep—
God's vicar in his twilight nursery dim,
  To gather us about the Saviour's knee—
  I saw a something fill their azure rim
That caught him worlds and years away from me;
  And like a javelin once more through me passed
  The pang that pierced me walking on the sea.
"O saints!" I cried, "must loss be still the last?"

XVII.

When I said this, the cloud of witnesses
  Turned all their faces sideways, and grew dim—
  So that I saw but half of their sweet bliss,
And dim as the old moon in the new moon's rim.
  But as I gazed, a thought—a gleam of light

On every outline 'gan to glimmer and swim,
Faint as the young moon, threadlike on the night,
  Just born of sunbeams trembling on her edge.
  Was it a smile that broke in luminous white?
Or did some dawn begin to drive a wedge
  Into the night, and cleave the clinging dark?
  There was no moon or star, token or pledge
Of light, save that one bordering silvery mark
  Outshaping to my eyes their vanished look.
  It swelled and grew. Suddenly—as a spark
Of vital touch had found some hidden nook
  Where germs of potent harmonies lay prest,
  Whose life outbursting straight the silence shook—
Rose in a jubilation calmly blest,
  From that great cone of faces a high song,
  Instinct with such harmonical unrest
That in a flood of weeping—" Lord, how long?"
  I answered it because I could not sing.

And as they sung, the light more clear and
    strong
Flamed on their faces, till I scarce could bring
    My eyes the radiance to encounter and bear;
    Light from their eyes, like water from a spring,
Flowed; on their foreheads reigned their flashing
    hair;
    And from their lips the great song floated free:
"O brother! sister! *he* comes! Love is there!"
Speechless I gazed, thinking—if it were He,
    Then——But the faces moved! those precious
    eyes
    Were turning on me! In rushed holy glee,
And woke me to the dark of lower skies!

XVIII.

As a captive, whom one clank of iron chain
    Drags down from dreams of bliss to bitterness,
    Stung with its loss, I called the vision vain,

Yet feeling life grown larger, suffering less,
    Dim-eyed, half-raised, I looked into the hush
    Of the room—veiled that morning should not
        press
Upon the slumber which had stayed the rush
    Of ebbing life: there sat one watching lone,
    And on her brow the dawn's first grayest flush.
One then was left me of the radiant cone !
    Its light on her dear face, though faint and wan,
    Was shining yet—a glimmer to me thrown
From the far coming of the Son of Man!

XIX.

In every forehead now I see a sky
    Catching the dawn; I hear the wintriest breeze
    About me blow the news—the Lord is nigh.
The night is long, dark are the polar seas,
    Yet slanting suns ascend the northern hill.

Round Spring's own steps the oozy waters freeze,
But hold them not.   Dreamers yet sleep their fill,
  But labourers, light-stung, from their slumber
    start.
  Faith sees the ripening ears with harvest fill,
When but green blades the clinging earth-clods part.

XX.

Lord, I have spoken a poor parable—
  In which I would have said thy name alone
  Is the one secret lying in Truth's well ;
Thy voice the hidden charm in music's tone ;
  Thy face the heart of every flower on earth ;
  Its vision the one hope ; for every moan,
Thy love the cure.   O sharer of the birth
  Of little children seated on thy knee !
  O human God ! I laugh with sacred mirth
To think how all the laden must go free ;

For though the vision tarry—in healing ruth
One morn the eyes that shone in Galilee
Shall dawn upon us, full of grace and truth.

THE SANGREAL.

[A part of the story omitted in the old romances.]

I.

How Sir Galahad despaired of finding the Grail.

THROUGH the wood the sunny day
    Glimmered sweetly glad ;
Through the wood his weary way
    Rode Sir Galahad.

All about stood open porch,
    Long-drawn cloister dim ;
'Twas a wavering wandering church,
    Every side of him.

On through columns arching high—
    Foliage-vaulted, he,
Rode in thirst that made him sigh,
    Like a misery.

Came the moon, through ghostly trees
    Glimmering faintly glad;
Withered, worn, and ill at ease,
    Down lay Galahad;

Closed his eyes, and took no heed
    What might come to pass;
Heard his hunger-busy steed
    Cropping dewy grass.

Cool and juicy was the blade,
    Good to him as wine;
For his labour he was paid—
    Galahad must pine.

Late had he, at Arthur's board,
  Arthur strong and wise,
Pledged the cup with friendly lord,
  Looked in ladies' eyes.

Now, alas! he wandered wide,
  Resting never more,
Over lake and mountain-side,
  Over sea and shore!

Swift in vision rose and fled
  All he might have had;
Weary tossed his restless head,
  And his heart grew sad.

With the lowliest in the land,
  He a maiden fair
Might have led with virgin hand
  From the altar-stair.

Youth away with strength would glide,
    Age bring frost and woe;
Through the world so dreary wide,
    Mateless he must go!

Lost was life and all its good—
    Gone without avail!
All his labour never would
    Find the Holy Grail!

II.

How Sir Galahad found and lost the Grail.

Galahad was in the night,
    And the wood was drear;
But to men in darksome plight
    Radiant things appear.

THE SANGREAL.

Wings he heard not floating by,
    Heard no heavenly hail;
But he started with a cry—
    Saw the Holy Grail.

Hid from bright, beholding sun,
    Hid from moonlight wan—
Lo, from age-long darkness won,
    And restored to man!

Three feet off, on cushioned moss,
    As if cast away,
Homely wood with carven cross,
    Rough and rude it lay.

Too much trembling to rise up,
    Reverent gazed the knight;
Fearing, daring, towards the cup
    Stole his hand of might.

But, as if it fled from harm,
   Sank the holy thing;
Eager following hand and arm
   Plunged into a spring.

Oh the thirst! the water sweet!—
   Down he lay and quaffed;
Quaffed and rose up to his feet;
   Rose and gayly laughed

Fell upon his knees to thank,
   Loved and lauded there;
Stretched him on the mossy bank,
   Fell asleep in prayer;

Dreamed, and dreaming murmured low
   Ave, pater, creed:
When the fir-tops 'gan to glow,
   Waked and called his steed;

THE SANGREAL.

Drew the girth, and loosed his sword,
   Braced his slackened mail;
Doubting said: "I dreamed the Lord
   Offered me the Grail."

III.

How Sir Galahad gave up the Quest for the Grail

Ere the sun had cast his light
   On the water's face,
Firm in saddle rode the knight
   From the holy place;

Merry songs began to sing,
   Let his matins bide;
Rode a good hour pondering,
   And was turned aside--

Saying, "I will wisely then
    Cease a hopeless quest
After dream of ancient men —
    Visionary Best!

"Common good than miracle
    Yields a better hold;
Grail indeed was that fair well
    Full of water cold.

"Not my thirst alone it stilled,
    But my soul it stayed;
And my heart, with gladness filled,
    Wept and laughed and prayed.

"Hidden church I seek in vale,
    Wood, or lake, no more;
I shall find a Holy Grail
    Where the need is sore."

IV.

How Sir Galahad sought yet again for the Grail.

On he rode, to succour bound,
 But his faith grew dim:
Wells for thirst he many found,
 Water none for him.

Never more from drinking deep
 Up he rose and laughed;
Never more a prayerful sleep
 Followed on the draught.

Common water, all they bore,
 Plentifully flowed;
Quenched his thirst, but ah! no more
 Eased his bosom's load.

For the *Best* no more he sighed—
  Saw the good askance;
Life grew poor and vague and wide,
  And his lot a chance.

Then he dreamed through Jesus' hand
  That he drove a nail;
Woke and cried, "Through every land,
  Lord, I seek thy Grail."

V.

That Sir Galahad found the Grail.

Up the quest again he took,
  Rode through wood and wave;
Sought in every mossy nook,
  Every hermit cave;

Sought until the evening red
   Sunk in shadow deep ;
Sought until the moonlight fled ;
   Slept, and sought in sleep.

Where he wandered, seeking, sad,
   Story does not say ;
But at length Sir Galahad
   Found it on a day ;

Took the cup into his hand,
   Held the Grail of joy :
Carried it about the land,
   Gleesome as a boy ;

Laid his sword where he had found
   Boot for every bale ;
Stuck his spear into the ground ;
   Kept alone the Grail.

VI.

How Sir Galahad carried about the Grail.

Horse and crested helmet gone,
    Mace and shield and mail,
He loud caroling walked on
    For he had the Grail—

Caroling walked south and north,
    East and west, for years;
Where he went, the smiles came forth,
    Where he left, the tears.

Glave nor charger needed he,
    Spur nor iron flail:
Evil might not brook to see
    Once the Holy Grail.

Winds he wandered with his staff,
    Woods no longer sad ;
Earth and sky and sea did laugh
    Round Sir Galahad.

Bitter mere nor trodden pool
    Did in service fail,
Flowing sweet and clear and cool
    From the Holy Grail.

Without where to lay his head,
    Chanting loud he went ;
Found each cave a palace-bed,
    Every rock a tent.

Age that had begun to quail
    In the gathering gloom,
Counselled he to seek the Grail,
    And forget the tomb.

Bright with hope, or passion-pale,
    Youths with eager eyes,
Taught he that the Holy Grail
    Was the only prize.

Maiden, worn with hidden ail,
    Restless and unsure,
Taught he that the Holy Grail
    Was the only cure.

Children, rosy in the sun,
    Ran to hear his tale—
How twelve little ones had won
    Each of them the Grail.

THE SANGREAL.

VII.

How Sir Galahad hid the Grail.

Very still was earth and sky,
    When in death he lay;
Oft he said he should not die—
    Would but go away.

When he passed, they reverent sought,
    Where his hand lay prest,
For the cup he bare, they thought,
    Hidden in his breast.

Hope and haste and eager thrill
    Were of none avail:
Hid he held it—deeper still—
    Took with him the Grail.

THE FAILING TRACK.

Where went the feet that hitherto have come?
   Here yawns no gulf to quench the flowing Past.
With lengthening pauses broke, the path grows
    dumb;
   The grass floats in; the gazer stands aghast.

Tremble not, maiden. Let the footprints die.
   No trodden way leads up the skylark's notes;
The mighty-throated, when he mounts the sky,
   Over some lowly landmark sings and floats.

Be of good cheer. Paths vanish from the wave
   Where thousand ships have torn their tracks of
    gray;
But ships undaunted still the desert brave:
   In each a magic finger points the way.

No finger finely touched, no eye of lark,
   Hast thou to guide thy steps where footprints fail?
Ah, then, 'twere well to turn before the dark,
   Nor dream to find thy dreams in yonder vale!

The backward path one hour is plain to see—
   Hapless wert thou, if that were lost behind!
Back to the prayer beside thy mother's knee—
   Back to the question and the childlike mind!

Then start afresh—but toward some noble end,
   Some goal o'er which hangs a known star all night;
So shall thou need no footprints to befriend:
   Child-heart and shining star will guide thee right.

TELL ME.

"Traveller, what lies over the hill?
　Traveller, tell to me:
Tiptoe-high on the window-sill,
　Over I cannot see."

"My child, a valley green lies there,
　Lovely with trees, and shy;
And a tiny brook that says—'Take care,
　Or I'll drown you by and by.'"

"And what comes next?"—"A little town,
　And a towering hill again;
More hills and valleys, up and down,
　And a river now and then."

"And what comes next?"—"A lonely moor,
    Without one beaten way;
And slow clouds drifting dull before
    A wind that will not stay."

"And then?"—"Dark rocks and yellow sand,
    Blue sea and a moaning tide."
"And then?"—"More sea, more sea, more land,
    With rivers deep and wide."

"And then?"—"Oh—rock and mountain and vale,
    Ocean and shores and men,
Over and over—a weary tale—
    And round to your home again!"

"And is that all? From day to day—
    As with a long chain bound—
Oh! never to get right away,
    But go round and round and round?"

"No, no; I have not told the best—
  Neither the best nor the end:
On summer eves, away in the west,
  You may see a stair ascend,

"Built of all colours of lovely stones—
  A stair up into the sky,
Where no one is weary, and no one moans,
  Or wants to be laid by."

" Is it far away?"   "I do not know.
  You must fix your eyes thereon,
And travel, travel, through thunder and snow,
  Till the weary way is gone.

" All day, though you never see it shine,
  You must travel, nor turn aside,
Through blinding sunlight and moonbeams fine
  And mist and darkness wide."

"When I am older." "Nay, not so."
  "I have hardly opened my eyes!"
"He who to the old sunset would go,
  Starts best with the young sunrise."

"But the stair—is it very very steep?"
  "Too steep for you to climb;
You must lie at the foot of the glorious heap,
  And patient wait your time."

"How long?" "Nay, that I cannot tell."
  "In wind, and rain, and frost?"
"It may be." "Ah!—ah!" "It is well
  That you should count the cost.

" Yea, travellers many on you will stand.'
  'That will be hard to bear."
" But one with wounded foot and hand
  Will carry you up the stair."

BROTHER ARTIST!

BROTHER artist! help me—come.
   Artists are a maimed band:
   I have words, but not a hand;
Thou hast hands though thou art dumb

Had I thine—when words did fail—
   Vassal-words their hurrying chief—
   On the white awaiting leaf
Shapes of power should tell the tale.

Had I hers, of music-might,
   I would rule the air with storm,
   Till the red clouds trailed enorm
Boreal dances through the night.

Had I his, whose foresight rare
   Piles the stones with kingliest art,
   From the quarry of my heart
Love should climb a heavenly stair.

Had I his, whose wooing slow
   Wins the marble's hidden child,
   Out in passion undefiled
Stood my Psyche, white as snow.

Maimed, a little help I pray—
   Words can only do a part;
   Let thy hand obey my heart;
Say for me what I would say.

Draw me—on an arid plain,
   With the rocky mountains nigh,
   Under a clear morning sky,
Telling of a night of rain—

Huge and rugged, like a block
   Chosen for sarcophagus
   To a Pharaoh glorious,
One rude solitary rock.

Cleave it down, along the ridge,
   With a yawning fissure—deep,
   Splitting all the granite heap—
Like the rent of riving wedge.

Through the cleft let hands appear,
   Pointing up, with joined palms,
   As if lifting silent psalms
For the daylight come anear.

Turn thee now—'tis almost done—
   To the near horizon's verge;
   Make the smallest arc emerge
Of the glory of the sun.

Once again—there is not much—
   From a forehead hopeful-brave
   Sweep the shadow of the grave
With a single golden touch.

Thanks, dear painter; that is all.
   If thy picture one day should
   Need some words to make it good,
I will answer to thy call.

AFTER AN OLD LEGEND.

The monk was praying in his cell,
    With bowed head praying sore;
He had been praying on his knees
    For two long hours and more;

When, in the midst, and suddenly,
    His eyes they opened wide;
And on the ground, behold, he saw
    A man's feet him beside!

And almost to the feet came down
    A garment wove throughout;
It was not like any he had seen
    In the countries round about.

AFTER AN OLD LEGEND.

His eyes he lifted tremblingly
   Until a hand they spied;
A cut from a chisel there they saw,
   And another scar beside;

Then up they leaped the face to find;
   His heart gave one wild bound—
One, and stood still with the awful joy--
   He had the Master found!

On his sad ear fell the convent bell:
   'Twas the hour the poor did wait;
It was his to dole the daily bread
   That day at the convent-gate.

A passion of love within him rose,
   And with duty wrestled strong;
But the bell kept calling all the time
   With iron merciless tongue.

He gazed like a dog in the Master's eyes—
    He sprang to his feet in strength:
"If I find him not when I come back,
    I shall find him the more at length!"

He chid his heart, and he fed the poor,
    All at the convent-gate;
Then wearily, oh wearily!
    Went back to be desolate.

His hand on the latch, his head bent low,
    He stood on the door-sill;
Sad and slow he lifted the latch—
    The Master stood there still!

He said, "I have waited, because my poor
    Had not to wait for thee;
But the man who doeth my Father's work
    Is never far from me."

Yet, Lord—for thou would'st have us judge,
   And I will humbly dare—
If the monk had staid, I do not think
   Thou would'st have left him there.

I hear from the far-off blessed time
   A sweet defending phrase:
" For the poor always ye have with you,
   But me ye have not always."

A MEDITATION OF ST. ELIGIUS.

Queen Mary one day Jesus sent
    To draw some water, legends tell;
The little boy, obedient,
    Filled full the pitcher from the well.

But as he raised it to his head,
    Heavy, with overflowing rim,
The handle broke, and all was shed
    Upon the stones about the brim.

His cloak upon the ground he laid,
    And in it gathered up the pool;*
Obedient there the water staid,
    And home he bore it plentiful.

            Proverbs, xxx. 4.

A MEDITATION OF ST. ELIGIUS.

Eligius said : "It is not good :
   The hands that all the world control,
Had there been room for wonders, would
   Have made his mother's pitcher whole.

"Yet some few drops for thirsty need,
   An ancient fable even, told
In love of thee, the Truth indeed,
   Like broken pitcher, yet may hold.

"Thy living water I have spilt :
   I thought to bear the pitcher high ;
     But on the shining stones of guilt
   I slipped—and there the potsherds lie !

"What will He say whose love will drink
   From poorest cup that love hath filled,
If here I sit on Sychar's brink,
   My pitcher broke, thy water spilled ?

"What will they do I waiting left?
   They looked to me to bring thy law;
The well is deep, and, sin-bereft,
   I nothing have wherewith to draw.

"Lord, in the garment of thy flesh
   Thou brought'st the living water first;
Gather to thee thy truth afresh,
   Afresh to flow for human thirst."

THE EARLY BIRD.

A LITTLE bird sat on the edge of her nest;
   Her yellow-beaks slept as sound as tops;
All day she had worked without any rest,
   And had filled every one of their gibbous crops,
Had filled her own quite over-full,
And felt like a dead bird stuffed with wool.

"Oh dear!" she sighed, as she sat with her head
   Sunk in her chest, and no neck at all—
Just like an apple on a feather bed
   Poked and rounded and fluffed to a ball;
"What's to be done if things don't reform?
I can't tell where there's one more worm.

PARABLE.

"I've had twenty to-day, and the children five
    each,
Besides a few flies, and some very fat spiders;
Who will dare say I don't do as I preach—
    I set an example to all providers;
But what's the use? We want a storm—
I don't know where there's a single worm.."

"There's five in my crop," chirped a wee, wee bird
    Who woke at the voice of his mother's pain—
"I know where there's five." And with the word
    He tucked in his head and went off again.
"The folly of childhood," sighed his mother,
"Has always been my especial bother!"

Careless the yellow-beaks slept on—
    They never had heard of the bogy To-morrow;
The mother sat outside, making her moan—
    "I shall soon have to beg, or steal, or borrow;

For I never can tell the night before
Where I shall find one red worm more.

The fact, as I say, was—she'd had too many,
    And sleepless of course, set it down to foresight:
A barn of crumbs—if she knew but of any!
    Could she but get of the world's worm-store sight!
The eastern sky was growing red,
Ere she laid her wise beak in its feather bed.

Just then, the fellow who knew of five,
    Nor troubled his sleep with anxious tricks,
Woke, and stirred, and felt alive;—
    "To-day," he said, "I am up to six;
But my mother feels in her lot the crook—
What if I tried my own little hook?"

When his mother awoke and winked two eyes
    As undecided as those of a mole—

Could she believe them? What a prize!—

He was dragging a huge worm out of its hole!—

From him the old truth had its new proverb-
form—

'*Tis the early bird that catches the worm.*

SIR LARK AND KING SUN.

"Good morrow, my lord!" in the sky alone,
Sung the lark as the sun ascended his throne.
"Shine on me, my lord; I only am come
Of all your servants, to welcome you home.
I have shot straight up, a whole hour, I swear,
To catch the first gleam of your golden hair."

"Must I thank you then," said the king, "Sir Lark,
For flying so high and hating the dark?
You ask a full cup for half a thirst:
Half was love of me, half love to be first.

There are some creatures as much to my taste,
Whose watching and waiting means more than
    your haste."

King Sun hid his head in a turban of cloud;
Sir Lark stopped singing, quite vexed and cowed;
But higher he flew, thinking, "Anon
The wrath of the king will be over and gone;
And his crown, shining out of its cloudy fold,
Will change my brown feathers to a glory of gold."

He flew—with the strength of a lark he flew;
But, as he rose, the cloud rose too;
And not one gleam of the golden hair
Crossed the dull depth of the unblest air;
And his feathers felt withered and worn and old,
For his wings had had no chrism of gold.

Outwearied at length, and throbbing sore,
The strong sun-seeker could do no more;

He faltered, and quivered, and dropped like a stone
Into his nest—where, patient, alone,
Sat his little wife on her little eggs,
Keeping them warm with wings and legs.

Did I say alone? Ah, no such thing!
For there was the cloudless, the radiant king.
"Welcome, Sir Lark!—You look tired: you see
Up is not always the best way to me.
While you have been singing so high and away,
I've been shining to your little wife all day."

He had set his coronet round her nest;
Its radiance foamed on her little brown breast;
And so glorious was she in russet gold,
That Sir Lark for wonder and awe grew cold;
He popped his head under her wing, and lay
As still as a stone till King Sun went away.

THE OWL AND THE BELL.

Bing, Bim, Bang, Bome!
Sang the Bell to himself in his house at home.
High in the church-tower, lone and unseen,
In a twilight of ivy, cool and green;
With his *Bing, Bim, Bang, Bome!*
Singing bass to himself in his house at home.

Like a glimmering ball of forgotten snow,
Sat the Owl on a shadowy ledge below:
"Pest on that fellow sitting up there!
Always calling the people to prayer!
He shatters my nerves with his *Bing, Bang, Bome!*—
Far too big in his house at home!

THE OWL AND THE BELL.

"I think I will move.—But it suits me well;
And one may get used to it—who can tell?"
So he slept again, and with all his might;
Then woke and snooved out in the hush of night,
When the Bell was asleep in his house at home,
Dreaming over his *Bing, Bang, Bome!*

For the Owl was born so poor and genteel—
What could he do but pick and steal?
He scorned to work for honest bread—
"Better have never been hatched!" he said.
So his day was the night—for he dared not roam
Till sleep had silenced the *Bing, Bang, Bome!*

When five greedy owlets chipped the egg,
He wanted two beaks and another leg;
And they ate the more that they did not sleep
    well:

"It's their gizzards," said Owless; said Owl,
"It's that Bell!"
For they quivered like leaves in a wind-blown tome,
When the Bell bellowed out his *Bing, Bang, Bome!*

But the Bell began to throb with the fear
Of bringing his house about his one ear;
And his people came round it, all in a throng,
To buttress the walls and make them strong;
A full month he sat, and felt like a mome,
For he dared not shout his *Bing, Bang, Bome!*

Said the Owl to himself, and hissed as he said,
"I trust in my heart the old fool is dead!
No more will he fright foolish mice with his bounce,
And waste my time in a double pounce!—
I'll see the corpse, ere he's laid in the loam,
And shout in his ear *Bing, Bim, Bang, Bome!*—

"Hoo! hoo!" he cried, as he entered the steeple —
"They've hanged him at last, the righteous people!
His swollen tongue lolls out of his head—
Hoo! hoo!—at last the old brute is dead.
There let him hang, the shapeless gnome—
Choked, with his throat full of *Bing, Bang,
Bome!*"

He fluttered about him, singing *Too-whoo!*
And flapped the poor Bell, and said, "Is that you?—
You that never would matters mince,
Banging poor owls, and making them wince?
A fig for you now, in your great hall-dome!
My *Too-whit* is better than your *Bing, Bome!*"

Still braver he grew, the downy, the dapper;
He flew inside, and sat on the clapper,
And shouted *Too-whoo!* The echo awoke,
Like the sound of a ghostly clapper-stroke:

"Just so!" he cried; "I am quite at home—
I will take your place with my *Bing, Bang,
Bome!*"

He hissed in the pride of his grand self-wonder;
He called the Bell's echo his own great thunder;
He sat the Jove of creation's fowl.—
Bim, Bang! went the Bell—and down went the
    Owl—
A fluffy avalanche, light as foam,
Loosed by the boom of the *Bing, Bang, Bome.*

He sat where he fell, as if he had meant it
Nor found any reason as yet to repent it.
Said the oldest owlet, "Pa, you were wrong—
He's at it again with his vulgar song!"
"Be still," said the Owl; "you are guilty of pride;
I brought him to life by perching inside."

"But why, my dear?" said his soft-plumed wife;
"You know he was always the plague of your
    life."
"I have given him a lesson of good for evil;
Perhaps the old ruffian will now be civil."
His look was righteous, he raised his comb;
The Bell bawled on *Bing, Bim, Bang, Bome!*

BALLADS.

BALLADS.

THE UNSEEN MODEL.

FORTH to his study the sculptor goes,
    In a mood of lofty mirth.
  "Now shall the tongues of my carping
      foes
  Confess what my art is worth:
In my brain last night the vision arose—
    And the next shall see its birth."

He stood like a god : with creating hand,
    He struck the formless clay :
"Psyche, arise," he said, "and stand ;
    In beauty confront the day.

I cannot find thee in any land—
　　I call thee: thou shalt obey."

The sun was low in the eastern skies,
　　When spoke the confident youth;—
All day, sweet Psyche, with hands and eyes
　　He wiled from the clay uncouth;
Nor ceased when the shadows came round like spies
　　That hang about the truth.

For he said, "I will do my will in spite
　　Of the rising dark; for, see,
She grows to my hand! The mar-work night
　　Shall hurry and hide and flee
From the glow of my lamp, and the making might
　　That passeth out of me."

In the flickers of the light the figure swayed,
　　In the shadows did melt and swim:

With tool and thumb he modelled and made—
    Nor knew that feature and limb
Half-obeying half-disobeyed,
    And mocking eluded him.

On, on, at the Psyche of his brain
    He modelled the livelong night;
The oil went low, and he trimmed in vain—
    The lamp would not burn bright;
But shimmering through the high roof-pane
    He saw the first of the light.

The dark retreated; the morning spread;
    The figures their shapes resume;
The plaster stares dumb-white and dead;
    A faint blue liquid bloom
Lies on each marble bosom and head;
    But to Psyche clings the gloom.

Backward he steps—he would see the clay;
  His visage grows white and sear :—
No beauty ideal confronts the day !
  No Psyche from upper sphere !
But the form of a lady gone to decay—
  Buried a lonesome year !

From maidenhood's wilderness fair and wild,
  He had drawn the Psyche bride;
Blown out the lamp of the trusting child—
  And in the darkness she died.
Now from the clay she sadly smiled,
  And the sculptor stood staring-eyed.

He had called his Psyche—nor saw her creep
  From a half-forgotten tomb ;
She has brought her sad smile—'twas all she could
      keep—
  Her eyes are left in the gloom:

High grace hath found him, to make him weep,
   And love is his endless doom.

At eve he did pine, and at dawning rue,
   And he haunted her form with sighs;
And as oft as his clay to a lady grew,
   The carvers, with dim surmise,
Would whisper—"The same shape glimmering through!"
   And—"Ever the sad blind eyes!"

THE HOMELESS GHOST.

Through still, bare streets, and cold moonshine,
   His homeward way he bent;
The clocks gave out the midnight sign
   As, bowed in thought, he went
Along the rampart's ocean line,
Where, high above the tossing brine,
   Seaward his lattice leant.

He knew not why he left the throng—
   Why there he could not rest;—
What something pained him in the song,
   And mocked him in the jest;

Nor why, the flitting crowd among,
One moveless moonbeam lay so long
   Athwart one lady's breast!

He sat him down with solemn book
   His sadness to beguile,
But ever he saw her pallid look,
   Her face too still to smile;
An hour he sat in his fireside nook,
And time flowed past like a silent brook,
   Nor a word he read the while.

Vague thoughts absorbed his passive brain—
   Of one that lonely dies;
Of one that longs, but longs in vain;
   Of a love that only sighs;
When a sudden spatter of drifting rain
Drove in a gust against the pane,
   Mixed with a sea-bird's cries.

He looked from the lattice : the misty moon
   Hardly a glimmer gave ;
The wind was like one that hums a tune—
   The first low gathering stave ;
The ocean lay in a sullen swoon,
With a moveless, meaningless, murmured croon,
   Like the moaning of a slave.

The wind, with a sudden and angry blare
   Howled from the watery west ;
The window shivers, the candles flare—
   Slumber and dreams were best.
He turned : a lady sat in his chair ;
To the shoulder one white arm was bare,
   And it lay across her breast.

She sat like a queen on a ruined throne ;
   Like a lily bowed with blight ;

In her eyes the darkness about was blown
  By flashes of liquid light ;
Her skin and her garment with whiteness shone ;
Back from her forehead loosely thrown,
  Her hair was black as night.

All wet it hung, and wept like weeds
  On her pearly shoulders bare ;
The pale drops glistened like glassy beads
  Caught in a silken snare ;
As the silver-filmy husk to its seeds
Her dank robe clings, and a form he reads
  Too shadowy yet too fair.

Doubting she gazed in his wondering face
  Till his blushes began to rise ;
But she gazed, like one in forgetful case,
  To something beyond his eyes ;

To something that love holds ever in chase,
To something that is, and has no place,
   But away in the thinking lies.

He ran, and he brought her a garment of wool,
   And a fur, warm, soft and dry;
Listless, she in the gathering pool
   Dropped them, and let them lie.
He piled the hearth with faggots full,
Till the flames, as if from a fire at Yule,
   Up the chimney went roaring high.

She spoke—and lovely to heart and ear
   Was her voice, though broke by pain!
Afar it sounded, though sweet and clear,
   As from outside in the rain;
From out in the mist and the night so drear,
It came like the voice of one in fear
   Of the answer she shall gain.

"I am too far off to feel the cold—
　Too cold to feel the fire;
It cannot get through the heap of mould
　That soaks in the drip from the spire.
Fur and wool in fold on fold,
Cerement of wax and cloth of gold,
　Kill not a frost so dire."

Her voice and her eyes and her cheek so white
　Thrilled him through heart and brain;
Wonder and pity and love unite
　In a passion of precious pain;
Her beauty possessed him with tearful might;
But while he trembled with strange delight,
　He seemed to be out in the rain.

Sudden she rose, and kneeled, and clung
　With her arms around his feet:—

"I am tired of being blown and swung
   About in the rain and sleet;
But better is torture than ease among
Horrors that may not be said or sung!—
   And I hate the mouldy sheet;

"For, ah, though a ghost, I'm a lady still!"—
   The youth recoiled aghast.—
Her eyes grew wide and pale and chill
   With a terror vague and vast.—
He caught her hand—a freezing thrill
Stung to his wrist; but with steadfast will
   He held it warm and fast.

"What can I do to save thee, dear?"
   At the word she sprang upright;
On tiptoe she stood—he bent his ear—
   She whispered—whispered light.

She withdrew ; she gazed with an asking fear :
Like one that looks on his lady's bier,
   He stood with a face ghost-white.

"Six times before," the lady said,
   "For my soul I have come to sue ;
As the last sear leaf in the sky decayed,
   Out of the twilight I grew;
But voices or laughter, in garden or glade,
Baffled me, drove me, a wind-borne shade,
   Out in the dark anew."

He shivered, he shook, he turned to clay,
   For the fear went into his blood ;
His face grew a dismal ashy gray,
   Through his heart crept slime and mud.
The lady stood in a still dismay,
Drooped and shrunk and withered away,
   Like a frozen half-blown bud.

"Speak once more!—Am I frightful then?—
    I live, though they call it death;
I am only cold.—Say *dear* again."—
    But scarce could he heave a breath;
Over a dank and steaming fen,
He floated, astray from the world of men,
    A lost, half-conscious wraith.

"The seventh, last time! Oh, save me!" The cry
    Entered his heart, and lay.
But sunshine was his, and a rosy sky,
    And the ghosts' moonlight is gray.—
As a feverous vision will flit and fly,
And without a motion elude the eye,
    She was standing three steps away.

And oh! her eyes!—refusal base
    The light in her eyes had slain—
Cold they grew in her pallid face!

And now, like a ghost of the brain,
She stood by the lattice, thought-moved in space--
With a backward-longing, a doleful grace;
And the lattice clanged with rain.

Faded or fled—she had vanished quite!
 The loud wind sunk to a sigh;
Pale faces without paled the face of night,
 Sweeping the window by;
To the glass pressed many a cheek of fright,
With the gleam of a doubtful decaying light
 From a dull and staring eye.

Whence did it come? from the sky or the deep—
 That faint long-cadenced wail?
From the closing door of the down-way steep?
 From his bosom or out of the gale?
From the land of dreams, or the land of sleep?

He knew not; but on in his bosom creep
    Low echoes that quaver and quail.

The clouds had broken, the wind was at rest,
    The sea would be still ere morn;
The moon had gone down behind its breast,
    Save the tip of one blunt horn;—
Could it be the bird without a nest—
Across the moon and her shine in the west,
    A thin white vapour borne?

He turned from the lattice; but ah! his room,
    With its ghost-forsaken chair,
Was empty and drear as a hopeless tomb,
    Sad and faded and bare;
Cold and wretched, and filled with gloom,
The sense of an overhanging doom,
    And an ever-haunting care.

He had turned a lady, and lightly clad,
　　Out in the stormy cold !
Was she a ghost ?—Divinely sad
　　Are the guests of Hades old !
A wandering ghost ? Oh, self-care bad,
Caitif and craven and cowering, which had
　　Refused her an earthly fold !

Ill had she fared, his lovely guest !—
　　A storm of passionate blame
Tore the courage that blenched the test
　　In a thousand shreds of shame ;
Bowed his head on his aching breast,
Shore the plume from his ancient crest,
　　Puffed at his ancient name.

He sickened with scorn of a fallen will,
　　With love and remorse he wept ;
He fell down and kissed the footprints chill,

And the track by her garment swept ;
He kneeled by her chair, all ice-cold still,
Dropped his head there, and moaned until
   With weariness he slept.

He slept until the flaming sun
   Laughed at the by-gone dark.
"A frightful dream!—but the night is done,"
   He said, "and I hear the lark!
All day he read. But the evening gun
With a booming terror his brain did stun,
   Like the jackal's nearing bark.

Followed the lion, conviction, fast,
   And the truth no dream he knew.
Many nights he was torn by the conscience-blast,
   But it stilled as the morning grew ;
And ere seven moons had come and passed,

His self-reproach aside he cast,
    And the truth appeared untrue.

Another lady whose love was guile,
    Had made his heart her boast;
In the growing glamour of her smile
    He forgot the lovely ghost;
But she gave him bitterness wrapt in wile,
For she was false as a crocodile,
    And her heart was a den of frost.

Then the cold white face, with its woe divine,
    Came back in the hour of sighs:
Is it to comfort those that pine
    The true old faces arise?
He dreamed of her, sang to her, prayed for a sign;
He wept for her pleading voice, and the shine
    Of her solitary eyes.

"With thy face so still, and thine eyes so bright,
  And thine air of solitude,
Thou holdest my heart in a cold delight,
  Lovely and sad and good;
Come to me, come to me, lady white
Come—for I dream of thee all night,
  And on thee all day I brood."

She came not. He sought her in churchyards old,
  In churchyards by the sea;
And in many a church, when the midnight tolled
  And the moon shone eerily,
Down to the crypts he crept, grown bold;
And nameless graves in valley and wold
  He haunted—but never came she!

Praying her pardon more and more,
  And her love at any cost,
He pined and sighed and longed so sore

That he looked like a creature lost;
Thin and ghost-like his body wore ;
He faded out at the ghostly door,
   And was himself a ghost.

But if he found the lady then,
   The lady sadly lost,
Or she had found among living men
   A love that defied the cost,
I know not, till I drop my pen,
And wander away from earthly ken,
   And am myself a ghost.

ABU MIDJAN.

"If I sit in the dust,
    For lauding good wine,
Ha, ha! it is just,
    For so sits the vine."

Abu Midjan sang, as he sat in chains,
For the blood of the red grape ran in his veins.
The prophet had said, "O Faithful, drink not,"—
Abu Midjan drank till his heart was hot;
Yea, he sang a song in praise of wine;
He called it good names—a joy divine,

The giver of might, the opener of eyes,
Love's handmaid, the water of Paradise;
Therefore Saad his chief spake words of blame,
And set him in irons—a fettered flame.
But he sang of the wine as he sat in chains,
For the blood of the grape ran fast in his veins.

    " I will not think
       That the Prophet said,
    Ye shall not drink
       Of the flowing Red.

    " 'Tis the drenched brain
       With an after-sting,
    That cries, *Refrain*,
      'Tis an evil thing.

    " But I will dare,
       With a goodly drought,

BALLADS.

To drink, nor spare,
   Till my thirst be out.

"For *I* do not laugh
   Like a Christian fool;
In silence *I* quaff
   The liquor cool—

"At the door of my tent,
   'Neath the evening star;
For, when daylight is spent,
   And Uriel afar,

"I see, through the sky,
   The emerald hills,
And my faith swells high,
   And my bosom thrills,

"For I see them hearken—
   The Houris that wait;
Their dark eyes darken
   The diamond gate;

"I hear the float
   Of their chant divine;
And my heart like a boat
   Sails thither on wine.

"Can an evil thing
   Make beauty more?
Or a sinner bring
   To the heavenly door?

"'Tis the sun-rain fine
   Would sink and escape
But is caught by the vine,
   And stored in the grape;

BALLADS.

"And the liquid light
   I drink again;
It flows in might
   Through my shining brain;

"I love, and I know,
   And the truth is mine;
For mine eyes out throw
   The light of the wine.

"*I* will not think
   That the Prophet said,
Ye shall not drink
   Of the flowing Red;

"For his promises, lo!
   They sevenfold shine,
When the channels o'erflow
   With the singing wine.

"But I care not, I!—'tis a small annoy
To sit in chains for a heavenly joy!"

Away went the song on the light wind borne;
His head sunk down, and a ripple of scorn
Shook the hair that flowed from his curling lip,
As he eyed his brown limbs in the iron's grip.—
But sudden his forehead he lifted high,
For a faint sound strayed like a moth-wing by·
And like beacons his eyes burst blazing forth,
For a dust he spied in the distant north :—
A noise and a smoke on the plain afar?—
'Tis the cloud and the clang of the Moslem war!
He sprung aloft like a tiger snared;
The wine in his veins through his visage flared;
He tore at his fetters in bootless ire;
He called the Prophet; he named his sire;
From his lips, wild-shouted, the Tecbir burst;
He leaped in his irons; the Giaours he cursed;

And his eyes, where the wrath-fires quivered and run,
Were like wine in the crystal 'twixt eye and sun.

  The lady of Saad heard the shout,
And his fetters ring on the stones about;
The heart of a warrior she understood,
And the rage of the thwarted battle-mood;
Her name, with the cry of an angry prayer,
He called but once, and the lady was there!

  "The Giaour!" he panted; "the godless brute!
And I like a camel tied foot to foot!
Let me go, and I swear, by Allah's fear,
At sundown I sit in this scoundrel-gear,
Or lie in a heaven of starry eyes,
Kissed by moon-maidens of Paradise.
O lady! grant me the death of the just!
Hark to the hurtle! see to the dust!"

ABU MIDJAN.

With gentle fingers, and eyes of flame,
The lady unlocked the iron blame;
Brought her husband's horse, his Abdon, out,
And his linked armour, light and stout;
Harnessed the warrior, and hight him go
An angel of vengeance upon the foe.

With clank of steel and thud of hoof,
Away he galloped; she climbed the roof.

Out of the dust-cloud flashes leap,
For the sickle-shaped sabres inside it reap,
With stroke reversed, the human swath—
And thither he gallops, the reaper of wrath!
Straight as an arrow she sees him go,
Abu Midjan, the singer, upon the foe;
Like a bird he vanishes in the cloud,
But the thunder of battle bursts more loud,
Mingled of crashes and blows and falls,

Of the whish that severs the throat that calls,
Of neighing and shouting and groaning grim :—
Abu Midjan, she sees no more of him ;
Northward the battle drifts afar,
On the flowing tide of the holy war.

Lonely across the desert sand,—
From his wrist, by the thong, hung his dripping
    brand—
Red in the sunset's level flame,
Back to his bonds Abu Midjan came.

"O lady, I vow, 'tis a mighty horse !
The Prophet himself might have rode a worse.
I rejoiced in the play of his knotting flesh,
As he tore to the quarry in Allah's mesh ;
I forgot him, and swept at the traitor weeds—
They fell before me like rushes and reeds,
Or as the tall poppies a boy would mow

Drop their heads to his unstrung bow;—
Fled the Giaour; the faithful flew after to kill
I turned—and Abdon was under me still!
Give him water, lady, and barley to eat;
Then haste thee and chain the wine-bibber's feet."

To the terrace he went, and she to the stall;
She tended the horse like a guest in hall—
Slow-footed then to the warrior returned.
The fire of the fight in his eyes yet burned,
But he sat in silence, and seemed ashamed,
As if words of boast from his lips had flamed.
She spoke not, but left him seated—bound,
Silent and motionless—on the ground.

But what singer could ever sit lonely long,
And the hidden fountain not burst in song?
Abu Midjan sang as he sat in chains,   [veins.
For the wine of the battle foamed wild through his

"Oh, the wine
Of the vine
　Is a feeble thing!
In the rattle
Of battle
　The true grapes spring,

" When on whir
O' th' Tecbir
　Allah's wrath flies;
And the Giaour
Like a flower
　Down-trodden lies;

" When, on force
Of the horse,
　The arm, flung abroad,
Is sweeping,

And reaping
  The harvest of God.

"They drop
From the top
  To the sear heap below;
Ha! deeper,
Down steeper,
  The infidels go!

"Azrael
Sheer to hell
  Shoots the foul shoals;
And Monker
And Nakir
  Torture their souls.

"But when drop
On their crop

The scimitars red,
And under
War's thunder
The faithful lie dead,

"Oh! bright
Is the light
On the hero slow breaking
Rapturous faces,
Bent for embraces,
Wait on his waking.

"And he hears
In his ears
The voice of the river,
Like a maiden
Love-laden,
Go wandering ever

"Oh! the wine
Of the vine
  May lead to the gates;
But the rattle
Of battle
  Wakes the angel who waits!

"To the lord
Of the sword
  Open it must;
The drinker,
The thinker
  Sits in the dust.

"He dreams
Of the gleams
  Of their garments of white:
He misses

  Their kisses—
   The maidens of light.

  " They long
  For the strong
   Who has burst through alarms—
  Up, by the labour
  Of stirrup and sabre—
   Up to their arms.

" Oh ! the wine of the grape is a feeble ghost ;
But the wine of the fight is the joy of a host ! "

  When Saad came home from the far pursuit,
An hour he sat, and an hour was mute.
Then he opened his mouth : " Ah ! wife, the fight
Had been lost full sure, but an arm of might
Sudden rose up on the crest of the war,
Flashed from its sabre blue lightnings afar,

Took up the battle, and drove it on—
Enoch sure, or the good St. John !
Wherever he leaped, like a lion he,
The fight was thickest, or soon to be ;
Wherever he sprang, with his lion cry,
The thick of the battle soon went by.
With a headlong fear, the sinners fled ;
We drove them down the steep of the dead ;
Before us, not from us, did they flee—
They ceased—in the depths of a crimson sea!
But him who had saved us, we saw no more ;
He had gone, as he came, by a secret door.
And strangest of all—nor think I err
If a miracle I for truth aver—
I was close to him thrice—the holy Force [horse!"
Wore my silver-ringed hauberk, rode Abdon my

   The lady arose, nor answered a word,
But led to the terrace her wondering lord.

There, song-soothed, and weary with battle strain,
Abu Midjan sat counting the links of his chain.

"The battle was raging—he raging worse:
I freed him,—harnessed him,—gave him thy horse."

"Abu Midjan! the singer of love and of wine!
The arm of the battle—it also was thine?
Rise up, shake the irons from off thy feet;
For the lord of the fight, are fetters meet!
If thou wilt, then drink till thou be hoar—
And Allah shall judge thee—I judge no more."

Abu Midjan arose. He flung aside
The clanking fetters, and thus he cried:
"If thou give me to God and his decrees,
Nor purge my sin by the shame of these—
Wrath against me I dare not store:
In the name of Allah, I drink no more!"

THE THANKLESS LADY.

IT is May, and the moon leans down at night
   Over a blossomy land;
Leans from her window a lady white,
   With her chin upon her hand.

"Oh, why in the blue so misty, moon?
   And why so dull in the sky?
Thou lookest like one that is ready to swoon,
   Because her tears are dry.

"Enough, enough of longing and wail!
   O bird, I pray thee, be glad;
Sing to me once, dear nightingale,
   The old song, merry mad.

"Hold, hold with thy blossoming colourless, cold,
    Apple-tree white as woe!
Blossom yet once with the blossom of old,
    Let the roses shine through the snow."

The moon and the blossoms they gloomily gleam,
    The bird will not be glad:
The dead never speak in the mournful dream—
    They are too weak and sad.

Listened she listless till night grew late,
    Bound by a weary spell;—
Clanked the latch of the garden-gate,
    And a wondrous thing befell.

Out burst the gladness, up dawned the love,
    In the song, in the waiting show;
Grew silver the moon in the sky above,
    Blushed rosy the blossom below.

But the merry bird, nor the silvery moon,
  Nor the blossoms that flushed the night
Had one poor thanks for the granted boon.
  For the lady forgot them quite.

LEGEND OF THE CORRIEVRECHAN.

Prince Breacan of Denmark was lord of the
    strand,
  And lord of the billowy sea;
Lord of the sea and lord of the land,
  He might have let maidens be.

A maiden he met with locks of gold,
  Astray by the billowy sea:
Maidens listened in days of old,
  And repented grievously.

Wiser he left her in sorrows and wiles.
  He went sailing over the sea,
And came to the Lord of the Western Isles:
  Now give me thy daughter, said he.

The Lord of the Isles he rose and said :
    If thou art not a king of the sea,
Think not the Maid of the Islands to wed,
    She is too good for thee.

Hold thine own three nights and days
    In this whirlpool of the sea—
Or turn thy prow and go thy ways,
    And let the sea-maiden be.

Prince Breacan he turned his sea-dog prow
    To Denmark over the sea.
Wise women, he said, now tell me how
    In yon whirlpool to anchor me.

Make a cable of hemp and a cable of wool
    And a cable of maidens' hair ;
And hie thee back to the roaring pool,
    And anchor in safety there.

The smiths for love on the eve of Yule
    Will forge thee three anchors rare;
Thou shalt gather the hemp, and shear the wool,
    And the maidens will bring their hair.

Of the hair that is brown thou shalt twist one strand,
    Of the hair that is raven another;
Of the golden hair thou shalt twine a band
    To bind the one to the other.

He gathered the hemp, and he shore the wool,
    And the maidens brought their hair,
To hold him fast in the roaring pool
    By three anchors of iron rare.

He twisted the brown hair for one strand,
    And the raven hair for another;
He twined the golden hair in a band,
    To bind the one to the other.

He took the cables of hemp and wool,
    He took the cable of hair,
And he hied him back to the roaring pool,
    And cast the three anchors there.

The whirlpool roared ; and the day went by ;
    And night came down on the sea.
But or ever the morning broke the sky,
    The hemp had broken in three.

The night it came down; the whirlpool it ran ;
    The wind it fiercely blew ;
And or ever the second morning began,
    The wool had parted in two.

The storm it roared all day the third,
    And the whirlpool reeled about ;
The night came down like a wild black bird—
    But the cable of hair held out.

Round and around with a giddy swing,
  Went the sea-king through the dark ;
And round went the rope in the swivel-ring,
  And round went the straining bark.

Prince Breacan he sat by the good boat's prow,
  A lantern in his hand :
Blest be the maidens of Denmark now !
  By them shall Denmark stand !

He watched the rope through the tempest black,
  A lantern in his hold :
Out, out, alack ! one strand will crack—
  And it is of shining gold !

The third morn, clear and calm, came out—
  Nor lord nor ship was there !
For the golden strand in the cable stout
  Was not all of maidens' hair.

THE DEAD HAND.

The witch lady walked along the strand ;
   Heard a roaring of the sea ;
On the edge of a pool saw a dead man's hand—
   Good for a witch lady.

Light she stepped across the rocks—
   Came where the dead man lay :
Now pretty maid, with your merry mocks,
   Now I shall have my way !

On a finger shone a sapphire blue
   Between six rubies red :
Come back to me, my promise true—
   Come back, my ring, she said.

She took the dead hand in the live,
   And at the ring drew she;
But the dead hand closed with its fingers five,
   And they held the witch lady.

Loud she cried, and abjured the deed;
   From her lips a prayer half broke;
If the dead man heard, he took no heed,
   But held like a root of oak.

With a deathly chill crept up the tide,
   And sure of her, made no haste—
Up to her knees, and up to her side—
   Up to her wicked waist.

Over the blue sea sailed the bride
   In her love's own sailing ship;
The lady she saw them across the tide,
   As it rose to her lying lip.

Oh! the hand of the dead and the heart of the dead
   Are strong hasps they to hold!
Fled the true dove with the false kite's new love,
   And left the false kite with the old.

SCOTCH SONGS AND BALLADS.

SCOTCH SONGS AND BALLADS.

ANNIE SHE'S DOWIE.

NNIE she's dowie, and Willie he's wae.
What can be the maitter wi' siccan a twae—
For Annie she's fair as the first o' the day,
And Willie he's honest and stalwart and gay?

Oh ! the tane has a daddy is poor and is proud,
And the tither a minnie that cleiks at the goud :
They lo'ed ane anither, and said their say—
But the daddy and minnie they pairtit the twae.

O LASSIE AYONT THE HILL!

O LASSIE ayont the hill,
   Come ower the tap o' the hill,
Come ower the tap wi' the breeze o' the hill.
   For I want ye sair the nicht.
   I'm needin' ye sair the nicht,
For I'm tired and sick o' mysel'.
   A body's sel' 's the sairest weicht :
O lassie, come ower the hill !

Gin a body cud be a thocht o' grace,
   And no a sel' ava !
I'm sick o' my heid and my han's and my face,
   O' my thochts and mysel' an' a'.

I'm sick o' the warl' an' a';
The win' gangs by wi' a hiss;
Throu my starin' een the sunbeams fa',
But my weary hert they miss.
 O lassie ayont the hill!
  Come ower the tap o' the hill,
  Come ower the tap wi' the breeze o' the hill;
 Bidena ayont the hill.

For gin I but saw yer bonnie heid,
 And the sunlicht o' yer hair,
The ghaist o' mysel' wad fa' doun deid,
 I wad be mysel' nae mair.
 I wad be mysel' nae mair,
Filled o' the sole remeid—
 Slain by the arrows o' licht frae yer hair,
Killed by yer body and heid.
  O lassie ayont the hill! &c.

My sel' micht wauk up at the saft fitfa'
   O' my bonnie depairtin' dame;
But gin she lo'ed me ever sae sma',
   I micht bide it—the weary same;
   Noo, sick o' my body and name,
Whan it lifts its upsettin' heid,
   I turn frae the cla'es that cover my frame.
As gin they war roun' the deid.
      O lassie ayont the hill ! &c.

But gin ye lo'ed me as I lo'e you.
   I wad ring my ain deid knell;
The spectre wad melt, shot through and through
   Wi' the shine o' your sunny sel'.—
   By the shine o' yer sunny sel',
By the licht aneth yer broo,
   I wad dee to mysel', ring my ain deid-bell,
And live for ever in you.

O LASSIE AYONT THE HILL!

O lassie ayont the hill!
  Come ower the tap o' the hill,
Come ower the tap wi' the breeze o' the hill,
  For I want ye sair the nicht.
  I'm needin' ye sair the nicht,
For I'm tired and sick o' mysel'.
  A body's sel' 's the sairest weicht:
O lassie, come ower the hill!

THE BONNY, BONNY DELL.

OH! the bonny, bonny dell, whaur the yorlin
    sings,
Wi' a clip o' the sunshine atween his wings;
Whaur the birks are a' straikit wi' fair munelicht,
And the brume hings its lamps by day and by
    nicht;
Whaur the burnie comes trottin' ower shingle and
    stane,
Liltin' bonny havers til 'tsel alane;
And the sliddery troot wi' ae soop o' its tail
Is ahint the green weed's dark swingin' veil!
Oh! the bonny, bonny dell, whaur I sang as I saw
The yorlin, the brume, and the burnie, an' a'!

THE BONNY, BONNY DELL.

Oh! the bonny, bonny dell, whaur the primroses
    wonn,
Luikin' oot o' their leaves like wee sons o' the sun;
Whaur the wild roses hing like flickers o' flame,
And fa' at the touch wi' a dainty shame;
Whaur the bee swings ower the white-clovery sod,
And the butterfly flits like a stray thoucht o' God;
Whaur, like arrow shot frae life's unseen bow,
The dragon-fly burns the sunlicht throu!
Oh! the bonny, bonny dell, whaur I sang to see
The rose and the primrose, the draigon and bee!

Oh! the bonny, bonny dell, whaur the mune luiks
    doon,
As gin she war hearin' a soughless tune,
Whan the flooers an' the birdies are a' asleep,
And the verra burnie gangs creepy-creep;
Whaur the corn-craik craiks i' the lang-heidit rye,
And the nicht is the safter for his rouch cry;

Whaur the win' wad fain lie doon on the slope,
And the gloamin' waukens the high-reachin' hope!
Oh! the bonny, bonny dell, whaur, silent, I felt
The mune and the darkness baith into me melt!

Oh! the bonny, bonny dell, whaur the sun luiks in,
Sayin', Here awa', there awa', haud awa', sin;
Sayin', Darkness and sorrow a' work for the licht,
And the will o' God was the hert o' the nicht;
Whaur the laverock hings hie, on his ain sang borne,
Wi' bird-shout and tirralee hailin' the morn;
Whaur my hert ran ower wi' the lusome bliss,
That, come mirk or come winter, nocht gaed amiss!
Oh! the bonny, bonny dell, whaur the sun luikit
  in,
Sayin', Here awa', there awa', haud awa', sin!

Oh! the bonny, bonny dell, whaur aft I wad lie,
Wi' Jeanie aside me, sae sweet and sae shy!

Whaur the starry gowans wi' rose-dippit tips,
War as white as her cheek an' as reid as her lips
Whaur she spread her gowd hert till sne saw that
    I saw,
Syne fauldit it up and gae me it a';
Whaur o' sunlicht and munelicht she was the queen,
For baith war but middlin' withoot my Jean!
Oh! the bonny, bonny dell, whaur aft I wad lie,
Wi' Jeanie aside me, sae sweet and sae shy!

Oh! the bonny, bonny dell, whaur the kirkyard lies,
A' day an' a' nicht, luikin' up to the skies;
Whaur the sheep wauken up i' the simmer nicht,
Tak a bite, and lie doon, an' await the licht;
Whaur the psalms roll ower the grassy heaps;
Whaur the wind comes and moans, and the rain
    comes and weeps;
Whaur my Jeanie's no lyin' in a' the lair,
For she's up an' awa' up the angels' stair!

Oh! the bonny, bonny dell, whaur the kirkyard lies.
Whaur the stars luik doon, and the nicht-wind sighs!

JEANIE BRAW.

I LIKE ye weel upo' Sundays, Jeanie,
    I' yer goon and yer ribbons an 'a ;
But I like ye better on Mondays, Jeanie,
    Whan ye're no sae buskit and braw.

For whan we're sittin' sae douce, Jeanie,
    Wi' the lave o' the worshippin' fowk,
That aneth the haly hoose, Jeanie,
    Ye micht hear a moudiwarp howk,

It *will* come into my heid, Jeanie,
    O' yer braws ye are thinkin' a wee ;
No a' o' the Bible-seed, Jeanie,
    Nor the minister nor me.

Syne hame athort the green, Jeanie,
   Ye gang wi' a toss o' yer chin ;
Us twa there's a shaidow atween, Jeanie,
   Though yer han' my airm lies in.

But noo whan I see ye gang, Jeanie,
   Eident at what's to be dune,
Liltin' a haveless sang, Jeanie —
   I cud kiss yer verra shune.

Wi' yer silken net on yer hair, Jeanie,
   I' yer bonny blue petticoat,
Wi' yer kin'ly arms a' bare, Jeanie —
   On yer verra shaidow I doat.

For oh but ye're canty and free, Jeanie.
   Airy o' hert an' o' fit !
A star-beam glents fra yer ee, Jeanie ;
   O' yersel' ye thinkna a bit.

Fillin' the cogue frae the coo, Jeanie,
    Skimmin' the yallow ream,
Poorin' awa' the het broo, Jeanie,
    Lichtin' the lampie's leme—

Turnin' or steppin' alang, Jeanie,
    Liftin' an' layin' doon—
Settin' richt what's aye gaein' wrang, Jeanie,
    Yer motion's baith dance and tune.

I' the hoose ye're a licht an' a law, Jeanie,
    A servant like him 'at's abune:
Oh! a woman's bonniest o' a', Jeanie,
    Doin' what *maun* be dune!

Cled i' yer Sunday claes, Jeanie,
    Fair kythe ye to mony an ee;
But cled i' yer ilka-day's, Jeanie,
    Ye draw the hert frae me.

OWER THE HEDGE.

I.

"Bonny lassie, rosy lassie,
    Ken ye what is care?
Had ye ever a thought, lassie,
    Made yer hertie sair?"

Johnnie said it, Johnnie seekin'
    Sicht o' Jeanie's face—
Luikin' i' the gairden hedge
    For an open place.

"Na," said Jeanie, pawky smilin',
    "Nought o' care ken I;
Folk they say the groosum carl
    Is better passit by."

OWER THE HEDGE.

"Licht o' hert ye are. Jeanie.
    As o' fit and han'!
Lang be yours sic wiselike answer
    To ony speirin' man!"

"It's no to seek what ye wad hae, sir,
    Though yer words are few;
Ye wad hae me free o' care, sir,
    'Cep' 'twas a' for you."

"Dinna mock me, Jeanie, lassie,
    Wi' yer lauchin' ee;
Gin ye had but gliff or notion
    What gaes on in me!"

'Troth, I'm no sae pryin', John!
    It's noucht o' my concern.
Wad ye hae me gang a speirin'
    What's intill yon cairn?"

"It's ill to bide; but ae thing, Jean,
  Ye canna help, my doo—
Ye canna haud my hert fra looin'
  At the hert o' you."

II.

JOHNNIE turned and left her,
  Listit for the war;
In a year cam' limpin'
  Hame wi' mony a scar.

Wha was that was sittin'
  On the brae her lane—
Worn and wan an' altert,
  But aih! sae like his Jean?

OWER THE HEDGE.

Her goon was black, her eelids
    Reid wi' greitin' sair :—
" Maid and wife and widow," quo' he,
    " In a towmond bare?"

Jeanie's hert played wallop,
    Kenned him or he spak :
" I thocht ye had been deid, Johnnie!
    Is't yersel' come back?"

" O Jeanie, are ye a widow
    Tell me in a breath ;
To see ye lost like me, lassie,
    I wad be unco laith."

" She canna be a widow
    That wife was never nane ;
But noo, gin ye will hae me, Johnnie,
    Noo I will be ane."

His crutch he flang it frae him—
He thochtna on his hairms—
But cudna stan' withoot it,
And fell in Jeanie's airms.

GAEIN' AND COMIN'.

WHAN Andrew frae Strathbogie gaed,
　The lift was lowerin' dreary;
The sun he wadna raise his heid;
　The win' blew laich an' eerie.
In's pooch he had a plack or twa—
　I vow he hadna mony;
Yet Andrew like a linty sang,
　For Lizzie was sae bonny!
　　　O Lizzie, Lizzie, bonnie lassie!
　　　Bonny, saucy hizzie!
　　　What richt had ye to luik at me,
　　　And drive me daft and dizzy?

Whan Andrew to Strathbogie cam,
   The sun was shinin' rarely;
He rade a horse that pranced and sprang—
   I vow he sat him fairly.
And he had gowd to spend and spare,
   An' a hert as true as ony;
But his luik was doon, his sigh was sair—
   For Lizzie was sae bonny!

      O Lizzie, Lizzie, bonny hizzie!
      Aih! the sunlicht's dreary!
      Ye're straucht and rare—ye're fause as fair!—
      Hech! auld John Airmstrong's deary!

A SANG O' ZION.

ANE by ane they gang awa;
The gaitherer gaithers grit and sma':
Ane by ane maks ane an' a'.

Aye whan ane sets doon the cup,
Ane ahint maun tak it up;
Yet thegither they will sup.

Golden-heidit, ripe, and strang,
Shorn will be the hairst or lang:
Syne begins a better sang.

TIME AND TIDE.

As I was walkin' on the strand,
    I spied ane auld man sit
On ane auld black rock ; an' aye the waves
    Cam washin' up its fit ;
His lips they gaed as gin they wad lilt,
    But his sang he cud only say ;
An' it was but an owercome, waesome and
    dreigh—
O' tne words he had nae mae :
" Robbie and Jeanie war twa bonnie bairns ;
    They played thegither i' the gloamin's hush :
Up cam the tide and the mune and the sterns,
    And pairtit the twa wi' a glint an' a gush."

"What can the auld man mean," quo' I,
  "Sittin' o' the auld black rock?
The tide creeps up wi' a moan an' a cry,
  An' a hiss 'maist like a mock.
The words he mutters maun be the en'
  O' some weary dreary sang—
A deid thing floatin' aboot in his brain,
  'At the tide will no lat gang."

"Robbie and Jeannie war twa bonnie bairns;
  They played thegither i' th' gloamin's hush:
Up cam the tide and the mune and the sterns,
  And pairtit the twa wi' a' glint an' a gush."

"Hoo pairtit it them, auld man?" I said
  "Was't the sea cam up ower strang?
But gin thegither the twa o' them gaed,
  Their pairtin' wasna lang.
Or was ane ta'en, and the ither left—
  Ane to sing, ane to greit?

It's unco sair to be sae bereft—
  But there's ither tides at yer feet."
"Robbie and Jeannie war twa bonnie bairns,
  And they played thegither i' th' gloamin's hush:
Up cam the tide and the mune and the sterns,
  And pairtit the twa with a glint an' a gush."

"Was't the sea o' space wi' its tide o' time?
  Sic droonin' 's waur to bide;
But Death's a diver, seekin' ye
  Aneath its chokin' tide;
An' ye'll gaze again in ither's ee,
  Far abune space and time."
Never ae word he answered me,
  But he changed a word in his rhyme:
"Robbie and Jeannie war twa bonnie bairns,
  And they played thegither upo' the shore:
Up cam the tide and the mune and the sterns,
  And pairtit the twa for evermore."

"May be, auld man, 'twas the tide o' change
    That crap atween the twa?
Hech! that's a droonin' awfu' strange,
    And waur than ane an' a'!"
He said nae mair. I luikit, and saw
    The lips nae mair cud gang;
Ane o' the tides had ta'en him awa'—
    An' ower him I croont his ain sang:
"Robbie and Jeannie war twa bonnie bairns,
    And they played thegither upo' the shore:
Up cam the tide and the mune and the sterns,
    And soutt tnem awa' throu a mirksome door!"

THE WAESOME CARL.

There cam a man to oor toon-en',
  An' a waesome carl was he;
Snipie-nebbit, and crookit-mou'd,
  And gleyt o' ae blinterin' ee.
Muckle he spied, and muckle he spak,
  But the owercome o' his sang,
Whatever the tune, was aye the same:—
  There's nane o' ye a' but's wrang.

> Ye're a' wrang, an' a' wrang,
> An' a'thegither a' wrang;
> There's no a man aboot the toon
> But's a'thegither a' wrang.

THE WAESOME CARL.

That's no the gait to fire the breid,
   Nor yet to brew the yill;
That's no the gait to haud the pleuch,
   Nor yet to ca the mill;
That's no the gait to milk the coo,
   Nor yet to spean the calf;
Nor yet to tramp the girnel-meal—
   Ye kenna yer wark by half!
      Ye're a' wrang, &c.

The minister wasna fit to pray,
   And lat alane to preach;
He nowther had the gift o' grace,
   Nor yet the gift o' speech.
He mind't him o' Balaäm's ass,
   Wi' a differ ye may ken:
The Lord he opened the ass's mou',
   The minister opened's ain.
      He's a' wrang, &c.

The puir precentor cudna sing,
    He gruntit like a swine;
The verra elders cudna pass
    The ladles till his min'.
And for the rulin'-elder's grace,
    It wasna worth a horn;
He didna half uncurse the meat,
    Nor pray for mair the morn.
      He's a' wrang, &c.

An' aye he gied his nose a thraw,
    An' aye he crook't his mou';
An' aye he cockit up his ee,
    And said—Tak tent the noo
We snichert hint oor loof, man,
    But never said him nay;
As gin he had been a prophet, man,
    We loot him say his say:
      Ye're a' wrang, &c.

Quo oor gudeman : The crater's daft !—
  Heard ye ever sic a claik?
Lat's see gin he can turn a han',
  Or only luik and craik.
It s true we maunna lippen till him—
  He's fairly crack wi' pride ;
But he maun live—we canna kill him—
  Gin he can work, he s' bide.
    He was a' wrang, &c.

It's true it's but a laddie's turn,
  But we'll begin wi' a sma' thing :
There's a' thae weyds to gaither and burn—
  And he's the man for a' thing !—
We yokit for yon heich peat-moss—
  There was peats to cast and ca' —
Weel rid, we reckon, o' him and his
  Lang tongue till gloamin'-fa';
    But we're a' wrang, &c.

For, losh ! or it was denner-time,
　　The toon was in a low !
The reek rase up as it had been
　　Frae Sodom-flames, I vow.
We lowst and rade like mad, for byre
　　And ruck war blazin' fell,
As gin the deil had brocht the fire
　　To mak anither hell !
　　　　'Twas a' wrang, &c.

And there, on-luikin', the carl stude,
　　Wi' 's han's aneath his tails ;
To see him maisthan' drave us wud,
　　We ill cud haud oorsels.
It's a' your wite ; I tauld ye sae ;
　　Ye're a' wrang to the last :
What gart ye burn thae deevilich weyds
　　Whan the win' blew frae the wast ?

THE WAESOME CARL.

Ye're a' wrang, an' a' wrang,
An a'thegither a' wrang;
There's no a man in a' the warl'
But's a'thegither a' wrang.

THE MERMAID.

Up cam the tide wi' a burst an a whush,
    And back gaed the stanes wi' a whurr,
Quhan the king's ae son cam walkin' i' the hush,
    To hear the sea murmur and murr.

Straucht ower the sea there slade frae the mune
    A glimmer o' cauld weet licht;
For ane o' her horns rase the water abune,
    Like a lamp across the nicht.

Quhat's that, an' that, far oot i' the gray,
    Atwixt the mune and the lan'?
It's the bonny sea-maidens at their play—
    Haud awa king's son, frae the stran'

THE MERMAID.

Ae rock stude lanely up, and—hoot !—
    The king's son he steppit ahin';
The bonny sea-maidens cam gambolin' oot,
    Kaimin' their hair i' the win'.

O merry their lauch whan they fun' the warm san',
    For the lichtsome reel sae meet!
Ilk ane flung her kaim frae her pearly han',
    And tuik till her pearly feet.

But the fairest she cam to the rock sae tall,
    And her kaim in a crannie she laid.
Aboot he staw, and the quhytit shall
    Awa' in his breist he hed.

The cluds grew grim as he watched their game,
    And the win' blew an angry tune:
Ane after ane, ilk ane tuik her kaim,
    To the sea gaed dancin' doon.

But ane, wi' hair like the mune in a clud,
   She soucht efter a' war gane.
Creepin' he staw, and watchin' he stude,
   Quhill 't was mirk wi' a rush o' rain.

Wi' glimmerin' han's, like a blessin' priest,
   She fun' aboot for her kaim;
Rock-still he stude quhill upon his breist
   Fell the han' o' the bonny sea-dame.

Wordless and cryless she sank at his feet,
   And lay like a wraith o' snaw
Vainishin' i' the win' and weet
   O' a wastin' wastlin thaw.

He liftit her, tremblin' wi' houp and dreid,
   And hame wi' his prize he sped;
And laid her saft, like a withered sea-weed,
   On a purple and gowden bed.

THE MERMAID.

An' a' that nicht, an' a' day the neist,
    She never liftit her heid;
Nae breezy breath ever billowed her breist—
    She lay like ane o' the deid.

But quhan at the gloamin' the sea-airs keen
    Blew into the glimsome room,
Like twa settin' stars she opened her een,
    And the sea-flooer began to bloom.

The king's son he kneelit aside her bed;
    An' afore the mune was new,
Careless and cauld she was wooed and wed;—
    But a winsome wife she grew.

An' a' gaed weel till their bairn was born,
    And syne she cudna sleep;
She wad rise at midnicht and wan'er till morn,
    Hark-harkin' the sough o' the deep.

Ae nicht whan the win' was ravin' aboot,
  And the winnocks war speckled wi' faem,
Frae room to room she gaed in an' oot,
  And she thocht o' her kerfen kaim.

She set her to luik, an' open she threw
  Kist, aumry, and siller box;
She spied it at last—and straucht they flew
  Her han's to her gowden locks.

She twistit them up wi' her pearly han's,
  An' in wi' her pearly kaim!
She's oot and she's aff ower the shiftin' san's,
  An' awa' to her moanin' hame!

Ae cry cam back frae the heavin' bay:
  He waukit, and was himlane!
Her nicht-robe lay on the marble gray,
  But the cauld sea-woman was gane.

He ran, and he spied the open box,
    And he sped to the sea sae black;
A' nicht he roamit the mainin' rocks,
    But at day-daw lanely cam back.

An' ever an' aye, i' the first o' the mune,
    Whan the win' blew frae the sea,
The desert shore up and the desert shore doon
    Heavy at hert paced he.

But never more on the sands to play
    Cam the maids o' the merry, cauld sea;
He heard their lauchter far oot i' the bay,
    But hert-alane gaed he.

THE YERL O' WATERYDECK.

The wind it blew, and the ship it flew;
    And it was "Hey for hame!"
      up and cried the skipper to his crew,
    "Haud her oot ower the saut sea faem."

Syne up and spak the angry king:
    "Haud on for Dumferline!"
Quo the skipper, "My lord, this maunnabe—
    I'm king on this boat o' mine."

He tuik the helm intill his han';
    He left the shore un'er the lee;
Syne croodit sail, an' east and south
    Stude awa' richt oot to sea.

THE YERL O' WATERYDECK.

Quo the king, "There's treason i' this, I vow;
   This is something un'erhan'!
'Bout ship!" Quo the skipper, "Yer grace
   Ye are king but o' the lan'!"   [forgets

Oot he held to the open sea
   Quhill the north wind flaughtered and fell,
Syne the east had a bitter word to say,
   That waukent a watery hell.

He turned her heid intill the north:
   Quo the nobles: "He s' droon, by the mass!"
Quo the skipper: "Haud aff yer lady-han's,
   Or ye'll never see the Bass."

The king creepit doon the cabin-stair
   To drink the gude French wine;
An' up cam' his dochter, the princess fair,
   And luikit ower the brine.

She turned her face to the drivin' snaw,
   To the snaw but and the weet;
It claucht her snood, an' awa' like a clud,
   Her hair drave oot i' the sleet.

She turned her face frae the drivin' win'—
   "Quhat's that aheid?" quo she.
The skipper he threw himsel' frae the win,
   And he drove the helm alee.

"Put to yer han', my lady fair!
   Haud up her heid," quo he;
"Gin she dinna face the win' a wee mair,
   It's the waur for you and me!"

To the tiller the lady she laid her han',
   And the ship laid her cheek to the blast.
They joukit the berg, but her quarter scraped
   And they luikit at ither aghast.

Quo the skipper: "Ye are a lady fair,
   An' a princess gran' to see;
But war ye a milkmaid, a man wad sail
   To hell i' yer company."

She liftit a pale an' a queenly face;
   Her een flashed, and syne they swam:
"And what for no to the lift?" she says—
   And she turned awa' frae him.

Bot she took na her han' frae the gude ship's helm
   Till the day began to daw;
And the skipper he spak, but what was said
   It was said atween them twa.

And syne the gude ship she lay to,
   Wi' Scotlan' far un'er the lee;
And the king cam up the cabin-stair,
   Wi' wan face and bluidshot ee..

Laigh loutit the skipper upo' the deck :
  "Stan' up, stan' up," quo the king;
"Ye're an honest loun—an' ask me a boon
  Quhan ye gie me back this ring."

Lowne blew the win'; the stars cam oot;
  The ship turned frae the north;
An' or ever the sun was up an' aboot,
  They war intill the firth o' Forth.

Quhan the gude ship hung at the pier-heid,
  And the king stude steady on the lan'—
"Doon wi' ye, skipper—doon!" he said,
  "Hoo daur ye afore me stan'?"

The skipper he louted on his knee;
  The king his blade he drew :
Quo the king, "Hoo daured ye contre me?—
  I'm aboord my ain ship noo!

"Gin I hadna been yer verra gude lord,
   I wad hae thrawn yer neck!
Bot—ye wha loutit Skipper o' Doon,
   Rise up Yerl o' Waterydeck."

The skipper he rasena: "Yer grace is great;
   Yer will can heize or ding;
Wi' ae wee word ye hae made me a yerl—
   Wi' anither mak me a king."

"I canna mak ye a king," quo he,
   "The Lord alane can do that;
I snowk leise-majesty, my man!
   Quhat the deevil wad ye be at?"

Glowert at the skipper the doutsum king,
   Jalousin' aneth his croon;
Quo the skipper, "Here is yer grace's ring—
   An' yer dochter is my boon."

The black blude shot intill the king's face—
    He wasna bonny to see:
"The rascal skipper! he lichtlies oor grace!—
    Gar hang him heigh on yon tree."

Up sprang the skipper an' aboord his ship:
    He caught up a bitin' blade;
He hackit at the cable that held her to the pier,
    An' he thocht it ower weel made.

The king he blew hard in a siller whustle;
    And tramp, tramp, doon the pier,
Cam twenty horsemen on twenty horses,
    Clankin' wi' spur and spear.

At the king's fit fell his dochter fair:
    " His life ye wadna spill!"
" Daur ye to sunder me and my hate?"
    "I daur, wi' a richt gude will!"

"Ye was aye to yer faither a thrawart bairn;
    But, my lady, I am yer king;
An' ye daurna luik me i' the face,
    For a monarch's anither thing."

"I lout to my father for his grace,
    Low on my bendit knee;
But I stan' and luik the king i' the face,
    For the skipper is king o' me."

She turned; she sprang upo' the deck;
    The cable splashed i' the Forth;
Her wings sae braid the gude ship spread,
    And flew east and syne flew north.

Now was not this a king's dochter—
    A lady that feared no skaith—
An' a woman wi' quhilk a man micht sail
    Prood intill the port o' Death?

THE TWA GORDONS.

PART I.

THERE was John Gordon and Archibold,
    An' a yerl's twin sons war they.
Quhan they war ane and twenty year auld,
    They fell oot on their ae birthday.

"Turn ye, John Gordon, fause brither o' me!
    Turn ye, fause and fell!
Or doon ye s' gang, as black as a lee,
    To the muckle deevil o' hell."

"And quhat for that, Airchie Gordon, I pray?
    Quhat ill hae I dune to thee?"
"Twa-faced loon, ye sall rue the day
    Ye get yer answer frae me.

"For mine will be looder than Lady Janet's—
   Lood i' the braid daylicht;
And the wa' to speil is my iron mail,
   No her castle-wa' at nicht."

"I speilt the wa' o' her castle braw,
   I' the roarin' win' yestreen;
An' I sat in her bower till the gloamin' sta'
   Licht-fittit ahint the mune."

"Turn ye, John Gordon—the twasum we s' twin;
   Turn ye, and haud yer ain;
For ane sall lie on a cauld weet bed,
   An' I downa curse again."

"O Airchie, Janet is my true love—
   I notna speir leave o' thee?"
"Gin that be true, the deevil's a sanct,
   And ye are no tellin' a lee."

Their swerds they drew, and the fire-flauchts flew,
    And they shiftit wi' wary feet,
And the blude ran doon, till the grund a' roon'
    Like a verra bog was weet.

"O Airchie, I hae gotten a cauld supper—
    Cauld steel—and never a grace!
Ae grip o' yer han', afore ye gang!
    And turn me upo' my face."

But he's turnit himsel' upo' his heel,
    And wordless awa' he's gane;
And the corbie-craw i' the aik abune
    Is roupin' for his ain.

PART II.

Lady Margaret, her hert richt gret,
　Luiks ower the castle wa';
Lord Archibold rides oot at the yett,
　Ahint him his merry men a'.

Wi' a' his ban', to the Holy Lan'
　He's boune wi' merry din;
Upon his shouther a Christ's cross,
　In his breist an ugsome sin.

But the cross it brunt him like the fire,
　Its burnin' never ceast;
It brunt in an' in, to win at the sin
　That lay cowerin' in his breist.

A mile frae the shore o' the Deid Sea,
   The airmy haltit ae nicht.
Lord Airchie was waukrife, an' oot gaed he,
   A walkin' i' the munelicht.

Dour-like he gaed, wi' doon-hung heid,
   Quhill he cam, i' the licht o' the mune,
Quhaur michty stanes lay scattert like sheep
   An' ance they worshipt Mahoun.

The scruff and scum o' the deid shore gleamt
   And glintit a sauty gray;
The banes o' the deid stack oot o' its bed—
   It lickit them as they lay.

He sat him doon on a sunken stane,
   And he sighit sae dreary and deep:
" The deevil micht rack my soul quhan I wauk,
   Gin he 'd lea' me quhan I sleep.

THE TWA GORDONS.

"I wad gie my soul for ever an' aye
    Intill en'less dule and smert,
Gin I cud but sleep like a bairn again,
    And cule my burnin' hert."

Oot frae ahint a muckle stane
    Cam a voice like a huddy craw's;
"Behaud there, Archibald Gordon," it said;
    "Behaud—ye hae ower gude cause."

"I'll say what I like," quoth Archibold,
    "Be ye ghaist or deevil or quhat!"
"Tak tent, Lord Airchie, gin ye be wise—
    The tit winna even the tat."

Lord Archibald leuch wi' a lood ha! ha!
    Eerisome, grousome to hear:
"A bonny bargain auld Cloots wad hae
    It has ilka faut but fear."

"Dune, Lord Archibald?" craikit the voice.

"Dune, Belzie!" cried he again.—

The gray banes glimmert, the white saut shim-
Lord Archie was himlane. [mert—

Back he gaed straucht, by the glowerin' mune,
   And doon in his plaid he lay;
And soun' he sleepit—for a ghaist-like man
   Sat by his heid quhill the day;

And quhanever he moanit or turnit him roun',
   Or his broo began to looer,
The waukin' man i' the sleepin' man's ear
   Wad rown sweet words o' pooer.

And the glint o' a smile wad quiver athort
   The sleepin' cheek sae broon;
An' a tear wad gether atween the ee-lids,
   And sometimes wad rin doon.

Aye by his lair sat the ghaist-brooit man,
 And watchit his sleep a' nicht ;
An' in mail rost-broon, wi' his vizor doon,
 Rade at his knee i' the fecht.

Nor anis nor twyis the horn-helmit chiel"
 Saved him by force or fraud ;
An' Airchie said, "Gin this be the deil,
 He's no sae black as he's ca'd."

But wat ye fu' weel, it wasna the deil
 That tuik Lord Airchie's pairt,
But his twin-brither John, he thocht deid and gone,
 Wi' luve like a lowe in his hart.

PART III.

Hame cam Lord Archibald, weary wicht,
 Hame till his ain countree;
An' he cried quhan his castle rase in sicht,
 "Noo Christ me sain and see!"

He turnit him roun': the man in rost-broun
 Was gane, he saw nocht quhair.
At tne ha' door, he lichtit him doon—
 Lady Margaret met him there.

Reid, reid war her een, but heich was her mien,
 And her words war sharp and sair:
"Welcome, Airchie, to dule and tene,
 And welcome ye s' get nae mair.

"Quhaur is yer twin, Lord Archibold,
    That lay i' my body wi' thee?
I miss my mark, gin he's liesna stark,
    Quhaur the daylicht comesna to see."

Lord Archibald dochtna speik a word,
    For his hert was like a stane;
He turned him awa'—and the huddy craw
    Was roupin' for his ain.

"Quhaur are ye gauin, Lord Airchie," she said,
    "Wi' yer lips sae white and thin?"
"Mother, gude bye, I'm gauin to lie
    Ance mair wi' my body-twin."

She ga'e a skreigh; but oot an' awa'
    Was Airchie or she cud speik;
He ran and he gaed quhill he came to the aik—
    Was ever heard tell the like?—

"God guide us!" cryit he wi' a gastit rair,
  "Has he lien there ever sin' syne?"
An' he thocht he saw the banes pykit and bare
  Throu the cracks o' the airmour shine.

"O Johnnie! my brither!" quo' Archibold,
  Wi' a hert-upheavin' mane,
"I wad pit my soul i' yer wastit corp,
  To see ye alive again."

"Haud there," quod a voice frae oot the helm—
  "A man suld heed quhat he says:"—
And the joints they grippit and tore the gerse,
  As up the armour rase:—

"Soul ye hae nane to ca' yer ain:
  Ye wadna slype yer debt?
The sleep it was thine, and thy soul it is mine—
  And, Lord Archibald, weel met!"

"Auld Hornie," quod Airchie, "twa words to that:
  My burnin' hert burns on; [pat,
And the sleep, weel I wat, was nae reek frae thy
  For aye I was dreamin' o' John.

"But I carena a crack for a soul sae black—
  Yer wull o' her ye s' get;
Ye may burn her breist intill her back,
  Gin my Johnny afore me ye set."

The gantlets liftit the visorne up—
  Airchie thocht to see Mahound;
But John keekit smilin' oot o' the helm :—
  "O Airchie, ye are found!

"Yer soul is mine, brither Airchie," he quod,
  "An' I yield it ye back again;
For never a deevil cam near ye, waur
  Nor a brither o' yer ain."

Doon fell Archibald on his knee
　On the ower-green, bluid-fed sod :
"The soul that my brither gies back to me
　Sall be thine for ever, O God."

THE LAST WOOIN'.

"O LAT me in, my bonny lass!
   It's a lang road ower the hill;
And the flauchterin' snaw begud to fa'
   On the brig ayont the mill."

"This is nae change-hoose, John Munro."
   "I'll ken that to my cost,
Gin ye gar me tak the hill the nicht,
   Wi' snaw on the back o' frost.

"What hae I dune to vex ye noo?"
   "Last Wodensday, at the fair,
Ye lichtlied me, tae side yer mou,
   An' ye needna come nae mair."

"I lichtlied ye?"—"Abune the glass.
 Foul-fa' the ill-faured mou
That made the leein' word to pass
 By rowin' 't i' the true!

"It was but this: I dochtna bide
 To hear yer bonnie name
Whaur muckle mous war openit wide
 Wi' lawless mirth and shame;

"And what I said was: 'Hoot! lat sit;
 She's but a bairn, the lass.'
It turned the spait o' words a bit,
 And loot yer fair name pass."

"Thank ye for naething, John Munro;
 My name can gang or bide;
It's no a sough o' drucken words
 Wad turn my heid aside."

THE LAST WOOIN'.

"O Elsie, lassie, be yersel'!
    The drift hooes cauld and thrang;
O tak' me in ae hoor, and syne
    I'll gaither me and gang."

"Ye're guid at fleechin', John Munro,
    For ye heedna fause and true.
Gang back to Katie at the mill—
    She lo'es sic like as you."

He turned his fit; she heard nae mair.
    The lift was like to fa';
An' Elsie's hert grew grit and sair
    At sicht o' the drivin' snaw.

She laid her doon, but no to sleep—
    Her verra hert was cauld;
And the sheets war like a frozen heap
    O' drift aboot her faul'd.

She rase fu' ear', and luikit oot:
  A' was ae win'in' sheet;
At door-cheek, nor at winnock-lug.
  Was ever a mark o' feet.

She crap for days aboot the hoose,
  Dull-fitit and hert-sair,
Aye keekin' oot like a frichtit moose—
  But Johnnie was na there.

Lang or the thow began to melt
  The ghastly waesome snaw,
Her hert was safter nor the thow,
  Her pride had ta'en a fa'.

And whan the wraiths war halflins gane,
  And the sun was blinkin' bonnie,
Oot ower the hill the maid wad gang,
  To hear aboot her Johnnie.

THE LAST WOOIN'.

Half ower, she cam intill a den
　O' snaw and slush and weet:
The Lord hae mercy on her hert!—
　It was Johnnie at her feet!

Aneth the snaw his heid was smorit,
　But his breist was maistly bare;
And 'twixt his hert and his richt han',
　Lay a lock o' gowden hair.

The warm win' blew, the blackcock flew,
　The laverock was in the skies;
The burnie ran, an' a bleatin' began,
　But Johnnie wadna rise.

The sun was clear, the lift was blue,
　The winter was awa' ·
Up cam the green gerse plentifu',
　The better for the snaw;

And warm it happit Johnnie's grave,
　Whaur gowden the ae lock lay;
But on Elsie's heid white grew the lave
　Or the barley's beard was gray.

ALL SOULS' EVE.

Sweep up the flure, Janet;
   Put on anither peat.
It's a lown and starry nicht, Janet,
   And nowther cauld nor weet.

It's the nicht atween the Sancts and Souls,
   Whan the bodiless gang aboot;
An' it's open hoose we keep the nicht
   For ony that may be oot.

Set the cheirs back to the wa', Janet;
   Mak ready for quaiet fowk.
Hae a'thing as clean as a win'in' sheet:
   They comena ilka ook.

There's a spale upo' the flure, Janet;
   And there's a rowan-berry!
Sweep them into the fire, Janet,
   Or they'll neither come nor tarry.

Syne set open the ooter door—
   Wide open for wha kens wha?
As ve come ben to your bed, Janet.
   Set it open to the wa'.

She set the cheirs back to the wa',
   But ane that was o' the birk;
She sweepit the flure, but left the spale—
   A lang spale o' the aik.

The nicht was lowne; the stars sae still
   War glintin' doon the sky;
The souls crap oot o' their mooly graves,
   A' dank wi' lyin' by.

They faund the door wide to the wa',
　　And the peats blawn rosy reid :
They war shooneless feet gaed in an' oot,
　　Nor clampit as they gaed.

There's ane o' them sittin' afore the fire !
　　Ye wadna hearken tc me !
Janet, ye left a cheir by the fire,
　　Whaur I tauld ye nae cheir suld be.

Janet she smilit in her minnie's face :
　　She had brunt the roden reid ;
But she left aneth the birken cheir
　　The spale frae a coffin-lid.

Saft she rase and gaed but the hoose,
　　An' ilka door did steik.
Three hours gaed by and her minnie heard
　　Sound o' the deid nor quick;

Whan the grav cock crew, she thocht she heard
    The fa' o' shuneless feet ;
Whan the rud cock crew, she heard the door,
    An' a sough o' win' and weet.

Whan the gowd cock crew, Janet cam back—
    Her face it was gray o' ble ;
She laid her doon by her mither's side,
    An she closit her dazed-like ee.

Her white lips had na a word to say,
    More than the soulless deid ;
Seven lang days and nichts she lay,
    And never a word she said.

But suddent as oot o' a sleep she brade,
    Smilin' richt winsomely ;
And she spak, but her word it was far and strayit,
    Like a whisper come ower the sea.

ALL SOULS' EVE.

And never more did they hear her lauch,
   Nor ever a tear doon ran;
But a smile aye flittit aboot her face,
   Like the mune on a water wan.

Ilka nicht atween Sancts and Souls,
   She laid the doors to the wa';
Blew up the fire, and set the cheir,
   And loot the spale doon fa'.

An' at midnicht she gaed but the hoose,
   Aye steekin' door and door.
Whan the gowd cock crew, quaiet as a moose
   She cam creepin' ower the flure.

Mair wan grew her face, her smile mair sweet,
   Quhill the seventh All Souls' Eve:
Her mother she heard the shuneless feet,
   Said, she'll be ben belyve

She camna ben.   Her minnie rase ;
   For fear she maist cudna stan' ;
She grippit the wa', and but she gaed—
   For the gowden cock had crawn.

Janet sat smilin' upo' the cheir,
   White as the day did daw ;
But her smile was a sunglint left on the sea,
   Whan the sun himsel is awa'.

END OF VOL. IV.

www.ingramcontent.com/pod-product-compliance
Lightning Source LLC
Chambersburg PA
CBHW031906220426
43663CB00006B/790